Praise for
Blessed Hour of Prayer

Only a hymn writer as prolific as Fanny Crosby could have enough material to inspire 365 daily meditations. And only a true hymn lover could curate her offerings so skillfully into this wonderful devotional guide. Gary Holloway has crafted thoughtful reflections on Crosby's best known hymns while also spotlighting wonderful, lesser known gems. In the process he reminds us once again how deep, beautiful and poignant the blind poet's work actually is. This collection is a loving, beautifully crafted treasure.

—**Randy Gill, D.M.A.**, Professor and Director of Worship Arts, Lipscomb University, Nashville, TN

***

If you have spent any amount of time in church, there's a high likelihood that you've heard, read, or even sung a lyric from a hymn by Fanny Crosby. In taking these deeply formative lyrics from Crosby and breaking them down for daily consumption, Gary Holloway has provided all readers with an incredible resource for daily study, prayer, and meditation.

—**D.J. Bulls**, Minister, Composer, Arranger, Hymnologist, Tyler, TX

***

Blind from infancy, the amazingly prolific hymnwriter, Fanny Crosby has blessed generations of believers with her powerful, poetic insights into the Christian life. Gary Holloway has mined the rich ore of Fanny Crosby's lyrics for devotional gems that will power your walk with God all year.

—**Randy Petersen**, author of *Be Still My Soul,* Co-author of *The One-Year Book of Hymns*

***

This devotional is a treasure. You will be blessed as you spend a few quiet moments each day with Fanny Crosby, a true sister of encouragement.

—**Shirley Raye Redmond**, author of the award-winning, *Courageous World Changers: Fifty True Stories of Daring Women of God.*

***

Gary Holloway has given us a wonderfully inspirational book of daily spiritual meditation. This compelling publication combines phrases from the hymns of Fanny Crosby with the biblical passages that inspired them. When we take time to meditate on these hymn texts and biblical texts they not only provide direction for the day, they encourage us to lift our eyes to the eternal city and the joys of heaven.

—**Jerry Rushford**, Curator, Rushford Center at Pepperdine University, leader of 20 Literary and Hymn Pilgrimages to Britain and Europe.

BLESSED HOUR OF PRAYER

365 DAILY DEVOTIONALS WITH FANNY J. CROSBY

By Gary Holloway

Published by KHARIS PUBLISHING, an imprint of KHARIS MEDIA LLC.

Copyright © 2025 Gary Holloway

ISBN-13: 978-1-63746-322-2

ISBN-10: 1-63746-322-7

Library of Congress Control Number:

All rights reserved. This book or parts thereof may not be reproduced in any form, stored in a retrieval system, or transmitted in any form by any means - electronic, mechanical, photocopy, recording, or otherwise - without prior written permission of the publisher, except as provided by United States of America copyright law.

Unless otherwise indicated, Scripture verses are taken from the HOLY BIBLE, NEW LIVING TRANSLATION, Copyright© 1996, 2004, 2007 by Tyndale House Foundation. Used by permission of Tyndale House Publishers, Inc., Carol Stream, Illinois 60188. All rights reserved. Used by permission.

Scripture taken from THE HOLY BIBLE, NEW INTERNATIONAL VERSION ®. Copyright© 1973, 1978, 1984, 2011 by Biblica, Inc.™. Used by permission of Zondervan

All KHARIS PUBLISHING products are available at special quantity discounts for bulk purchase for sales promotions, premiums, fund-raising, and educational needs. For details, contact:
Kharis Media LLC
Tel: 1-630-909-3405
support@kharispublishing.com
www.kharispublishing.com

To Danny Gregg, and to all who lead God's people in worship

CONTENTS

INTRODUCTION ix
JANUARY 13
FEBRUARY 45
MARCH 74
APRIL 105
MAY 135
JUNE 166
JULY 196
AUGUST 227
SEPTEMBER 258
OCTOBER 288
NOVEMBER 319
DECEMBER 349
INDEX OF HYMNS 380

INTRODUCTION

Next to the Bible, nothing has shaped our faith as Christians more than the hymns we sing. At any time of any day, the words of a gospel song or hymn can enter our minds, bringing reflection, challenge, and joy. This is why Alexander Campbell called hymns, "our creed in meter," that is, the way we confess our faith and the words that shape that confession.

This is an invitation to experience daily the words of the most prolific hymn writer in history, Fanny J. Crosby. By reflecting each day on one of her over 8,000 hymns and on the biblical verses that inspired them, we will be led into a deeper experience of the Jesus we long to see.

THE LIFE OF FANNY J. CROSBY

She was born in Southeast, New York, on March 24, 1820, into a family with deep roots in American history. At age six weeks she had an eye inflammation. Since her usual physician was unavailable, the family called an unfamiliar practitioner who placed poultices on her eyes, resulting in her lifelong blindness. Writing much later in life, she said she felt no resentment toward the man because "I have always believed since youth to this very moment that the good Lord, in His Infinite Mercy, by this means consecrated me to the work that I am still permitted to do."

Until age fifteen she was schooled at home, much of her education being memorization of the Bible. In 1835, she moved to New York City to attend the New York Institution for the Blind. After eleven years as a pupil there, she then became an instructor. It was also there that she became an accomplished musician, not only composing lyrics but learning to play the piano, organ, harp, and guitar. In her own words, "It has always been my favorite theory that the blind can accomplish nearly anything that may be done by those who can see."

And what accomplishments she had! She began by writing hymns used in the Sunday School movement throughout the United States. Unlike Sunday Schools today which are for the children of a particular congregation, the

Sunday School movement was designed to teach literacy to poor children (and later adults) who could not afford schooling. They were taught to read the Bible. Crosby's hymns helped in that effort.

Soon her hymns were being sung in Christian churches. She was asked to speak in many churches—Episcopal, Presbyterian, Methodist, and others—at a time when few women were allowed to do so. Her hymns also made her a co-worker of the most famous preachers of her day—Charles Grandison Finney, Henry Ward Beecher, and Dwight L Moody. She had a long-time collaboration with Moody's song leader, Ira David Sankey, who composed tunes for her hymns.

Next to her hymn writing, Cosby's greatest contribution was to the poor of New York through her work in Rescue Missions. In the 19th century, over one hundred of these Christian missions, alongside other Christian groups like the YMCA, cared for the needy of the city, long before there were government programs to assist them. Crosby spent many hours in those missions, caring for the poor as well as raising money for their ministries.

She lived a long and fruitful life, dying on February 12, 1915. To read more on her life, see *Fanny J. Crosby : an Autobiography* (Grand Rapids: Baker Book House, 1986, ©1906) and Edith L. Blumhofer, *Her Heart Can See: The Life and Hymns of Fanny J. Crosby* (Grand Rapids: Eerdmans, 2005).

How to Use This Devotional Guide

Fanny J. Crosby will always be known for her hymns. These gospel songs, found in every hymnal published since her time, have found their way into the hearts of Christians throughout the world. Not an hour goes by without someone singing those words. Some of the hymns found here will be familiar to you. Others may be new. Since her time, some have criticized her words as too sentimental and nostalgic. However, they call even those of us who have been Christians for decades back to a simpler, childlike trust.

This devotional guide is based on two firm convictions. First, that God is at work within us and among us. Secondly, we are not the first God has worked within and among. Each daily devotional here brings you in touch with the faith of Fanny Crosby and with those who for over two centuries have experienced God through her words. Each begins with a portion of one of her hymns, giving a direction for the day, a signpost of how God is working in us. It continues with an invitation to hear God's voice from a Bible verse on that theme. This allows us to hear God's voice in his word, the Bible, and let God shape our day and our lives. A brief meditation on that theme follows. The hymn, scripture, and meditation are meant to be read slowly, reflected upon, and taken as our "to be" and "to do" lists for the day. A brief prayer thought ends each devotional.

Thus this book can lead you into a time alone with God each day. This can be a devotion lasting a few minutes or it can be extended by singing the hymn and by examining the scripture passage in its wider context. The short prayer can also act are a prayer starter that leads you into a longer and deeper period of prayer.

This approach can also shape family worship or small group study. If each member of the family or group has already reflected on that day's devotion, then each can share the word they heard from God that day. This will lead to a time of group meditation.

This book might also be used in those planning worship, whether short devotionals or congregational services. To help in that planning, at the end of this book is an index of the hymns used in this book and the dates they were used. One can then use the scripture, meditation, and prayer for those days in worship planning.

A Word of Encouragement

There are no shortcuts in the life of the Spirit. Five to ten minutes a day alone with God will not automatically make one spiritual. However, it is a start. God will honor our intentions and work in ways beyond our imaginations if we make the time daily to be with him.

If you do not make that time now, I encourage you to begin. I believe your experience will be the same as mine in compiling this book. At first, it was a thrill and a joy to reflect on the hymns of Fanny J. Crosby, to meditate on a Bible verse, and to hear the voice of God. However, after a while, it became so daily. But it is in sticking to our pledge to be alone with God each day, particularly when we are busy or we don't feel like it, that we receive a greater blessing. I am struck by how often the blind Fanny Crosby spoke in her hymns of seeing Jesus and God. That is the heartfelt request of our daily prayer with him. That is the song Crosby teaches us to sing.

God calls us his beloved children. He wants to spend time with us. My prayer is that this book can be a tool to help you enjoy quiet, holy moments with Him.

JANUARY 1

HYMN

A little talk with Jesus,
Alone in secret prayer,
It gives me strength and courage,
Life's many toils to bear;
And though I sometimes falter,
Because the way is dim,
There is nothing can cheer me onward
Like a little talk with Him.

SCRIPTURE

But Jesus often withdrew to the wilderness for prayer (Luke 5:16).

MEDITATION

Jesus, the Son of God, felt the need to be alone with God. He developed the habit of making time to be with his Father. He did this because he knew he could not face the challenges of his life without strength and guidance from above.

If Jesus felt this need, how much more do we? Life is full of work that is beyond our strength. We cannot see the way we should go. But if we develop the habit of spending time alone with God, then we receive strength, courage, and joy.

And Jesus prays with us! That's why we say, "In Jesus' name," when we pray. The one who knows what it is like to rely on God is the one who hears our heartfelt cries. That little talk with Jesus sets the tone for the day. This is an invitation to have that daily talk with him. To speak from the heart. To listen to the one who loves you.

As we speak and listen, we also sing. We share a song with the most prolific hymn writer in history and with the countless Christians through the years that have sung her words.

"Lord Jesus, cheer us today in our talk with you."

JANUARY

2

HYMN

Blessed assurance, Jesus is mine!

Oh, what a foretaste of glory divine!

Heir of salvation, purchase of God,

born of his Spirit, washed in his blood

SCRIPTURE

I have written this to you who believe in the name of the Son of God, so that you may know you have eternal life (1 John 5:13).

MEDITATION

I grew up in a church where I heard little assurance of salvation, at least from the sermons. But I did hear the encouraging words of this hymn, "Blessed Assurance." That's why these words still mean so much to me.

And I heard the basis of that assurance, "Jesus is mine." Our certainty of salvation is not based on sinning less or knowing or getting our act together. It is based solely on trusting what God has done in Jesus.

What has he done? He has adopted us into his family and made us his heirs. He has bought us with the precious blood of Christ, washing us clean. And he has given us new birth through his Spirit. When we doubt our salvation, let us say, "Jesus is mine!"

"Lord Jesus, you are mine! May we taste your glory this day."

JANUARY 3

HYMN

Perfect communion, perfect delight,

visions of rapture now burst on my sight.

Angels descending bring from above

echoes of mercy, whispers of love.

SCRIPTURE

No eye has seen, no ear has heard, and no mind has imagined what God has prepared for those who love him (1 Corinthians 2:9).

MEDITATION

What will it be like to see the face of God? We cannot imagine the joy, the peace, the deepest satisfaction of that moment.

But even now we have glimpses of his glory. Through the work of Jesus, we have communion with the Father, Son, and Spirit. We see God's beauty in flowers, trees, mountains, animals, and sky. We delight in the love of family and friends, feeling the love of God there.

And there are angels. Unseen messengers from the Lord bring echoes of mercy, whispers of love.

When days seem so ordinary, we are sure of the visions of God we see by faith.

"Lord, open our eyes so we may see you this day. Open our ears to your words of love."

JANUARY 4

HYMN

Perfect submission, all is at rest.

I in my Savior am happy and bless'd,

watching and waiting, looking above,

filled with his goodness, lost in his love.

SCRIPTURE

Submit yourselves, then, to God (James 4:7, NIV).

MEDITATION

Submission is hard. Especially hard for those who grew up with a heritage of individual freedom. We were taught not to bow the knee to kings, or rulers, or any authority but our own,

Submission is hard. But not for those who have the blessed assurance of Jesus. For us, submission comes easy. It is a rest. We are in our Savior, and he is in us. Yet submission requires patience. We do not yet have the fullness of his presence. Even now, as we watch and wait for him, we are lost in his goodness and love.

So whatever happens today, no matter how painful the submission and watching and waiting may be, we are happy and blessed.

"Savior, give us perfect submission to you, so we may know the joy of your love."

JANUARY
5

HYMN

This is my story, this is my song, praising my Savior all the day long.

This is my story, this is my song, praising my Savior all the day long.

SCRIPTURE

That is why I can never stop praising you; I declare your glory all day long (Psalm 71:8).

MEDITATION

"What's your story?"

It is a question we often ask others, and they ask us. Perhaps we do not ask in those words, but we want to know who people are and we want them to know us.

What is your story? Who are you? We often answer that question by telling about our family or giving our autobiographies or bragging about our accomplishments. For those who have the blessed assurance of Jesus, that is our story. "Jesus is mine" summarizes all that we are. He is our family, our beloved brother. He is the main character in our autobiography, not us. He is the one who has accomplished all that we are and all that we have done.

And we do not only tell that story, but we also sing it.

"Lord Jesus, grant that we may praise you with every action and every breath."

JANUARY 6

HYMN

O let your light, tho' little, shine out,
Our Lord's command fulfilling,
To live for Him wherever we go,
And seek His will to do.

SCRIPTURE

In the same way, let your good deeds shine out for all to see, so that everyone will praise your heavenly Father (Matthew 5:16).

MEDITATION

Where I live, the sun sets before five P.M. in January. We long for more light.

It's not just January. We live in a world of darkness—violence, war, injustice, and poverty. A world of darkness needs more light.

There seems to be little we can do to bring peace and justice to the dark world. We are little people in one corner of the big world. But God is light. His power fills us. We are called to let our little light shine by seeking daily to do his will. A little light can brighten the darkest place.

"Lord, shine through us this day, that we might light the way for others."

JANUARY 7

HYMN

O let your light shine steadily on,   May glorify your Father above,

That all the world, beholding,   And praise His boundless love.

SCRIPTURE

Jesus spoke to the people once more and said, "I am the light of the world. If you follow me, you won't have to walk in darkness, because you will have the light that leads to life" (John 8:12).

MEDITATION

Enlightenment. We think of it in terms like "understanding" or even "education." Enlightenment usually refers to something we humans achieve by earnest effort. Enlightenment is a goal or an accomplishment.

We Christians believe that enlightenment is not an impersonal goal but is embodied in a human being, Jesus the Messiah. He is the light. By following him, we are enlightened not by some detached understanding, but by his light living in us through his Holy Spirit.

We live in the light of Jesus. By doing so, we shine the light on God the Father. By this light we show others how to praise and glorify God. And that light in us gives light to the world.

"Jesus, enlighten us so we may show your light of life to the world."

JANUARY

8

HYMN

O let your light shine cheerfully on,

When cloud and storm are breaking,

Its beams may lead some sorrow-oppressed

To yonder Ark of Rest.

SCRIPTURE

For this light within you produces only what is good and right and true (Ephesians 5:9).

MEDITATION

The news, movies, television shows, and books of our time are awfully dark. Movies about the future used to be optimistic—we were headed toward a great big beautiful tomorrow. Futuristic movies today focus on dysfunctional, crowded, and violent cities.

It's not only our culture that is dark. Many people we know are struggling with darkness in their lives. All they can foresee is struggle, pain, and death.

We are called to shine the light of Jesus that leads them to a place of safety, meaning, and rest. This day, let your light shine by small acts of kindness. Do what is good and right and true. Someone is looking for that light.

"Lord Jesus, grant that we might show the light instead of simply cursing the darkness."

JANUARY
9

HYMN

O let your light shine peacefully on

Till earthly cares are ended,

And night and gloom shall vanish away

In joy's eternal day.

SCRIPTURE

And there will be no night there—no need for lamps or sun—for the Lord God will shine on them. And they will reign forever and ever (Revelation 22:5).

MEDITATION

Letting our light shine may sound like shallow optimism. But we are not just giving a cheerful spin to events, ignoring the darkness of the world. Instead, our light reflects the overall story of the Bible. There is a God who in the beginning said, "Let there be light" (Genesis 1:3). The light was good. But darkness entered the world through sin.

God sent his light again by becoming flesh, the light of the world. Even death could not extinguish the light of Jesus. Yet, for now, the darkness persists along with the light. "The light shines in the darkness and the darkness can never extinguish it" (John 1:3).

But the time is coming when there is nothing but light. There will be no night. The light of the one who is Love will shine on us forever. This is the joyous day we proclaim.

"Loving God, may we share the hope of the eternal joyous day to come."

JANUARY 10

HYMN

Pass me not, O gentle Savior, / Hear my humble cry; / While on others Thou art calling, / Do not pass me by.

SCRIPTURE

A blind beggar named Bartimaeus (son of Timaeus) was sitting beside the road. When Bartimaeus heard that Jesus of Nazareth was nearby, he began to shout, "Jesus, Son of David, have mercy on me!" (Mark 10:46-47).

MEDITATION

Bartimaeus was desperate. He knew the healer Jesus could give him sight. But what if he missed Jesus? What if Jesus passed him by?

So Bartimaeus shouted. People told him to be quiet. He shouted even louder. And Jesus heard him, stopped, and gave him his sight.

Are we desperate enough to cry out to Jesus? Or do we think we can handle most things ourselves? Do we think we see when we are really blind?

"Lord Jesus, gentle Savior, do not pass me by."

JANUARY 11

HYMN

Let me at Thy throne of mercy   Kneeling there in deep contrition;
Find a sweet relief,   Help my unbelief.

SCRIPTURE

The father instantly cried out, "I do believe, but help me overcome my unbelief!" (Mark 9:24)

MEDITATION

This father was frantic. His son was demon-possessed. The demon often tried to kill his son. But the father heard that the disciples of Jesus could cast out demons. He goes and asks them to do so. They try. They cannot.

Then Jesus arrives. The frantic father is not sure that anyone can help his son. Still, he says to Jesus, "Have mercy on us and help us, if you can." "What do you mean, 'If I can'?" Jesus asked. "Anything is possible if a person believes."

The father makes the confession that I often make. And Jesus frees his son from the demon. He can free us if we trust.

"Lord, I believe! Help me overcome my unbelief."

JANUARY
12

HYMN

Trusting only in Thy merit, / Would I seek Thy face; / Heal my wounded, broken spirit, / Save me by Thy grace.

SCRIPTURE

The Lord is close to the brokenhearted; he rescues those whose spirits are crushed (Psalm 34:18).

MEDITATION

It doesn't take much to crush our spirits. A setback at work. A hurtful word. A hateful look. Or even the ordinary conflicts of life.

Then there are the big events that demolish our spirits and break our hearts. Failure. Disease. Pain. Disappointment. Death.

On ordinary days and terrible days, the gentle Savior is near. By his grace he saves. He heals our wounds. He revives our spirit.

We are only asked to trust his merit. To seek his face. To focus on Jesus, not on our misery.

"Lord, be close to me this day. Show me your face."

JANUARY
13

HYMN

Thou the Spring of all my comfort,

More than life to me,

Whom have I on earth beside Thee?

Whom in Heav'n but Thee?

SCRIPTURE

For the more we suffer for Christ, the more God will shower us with his comfort through Christ (2 Corinthians 1:5).

MEDITATION

If there's one thing I like it is comfort. I live in a comfortable house, warm in the winter and cool in the summer. I like to sit in my comfortable chair. I drive a comfortable car. Even financially, I would say that I am not rich but comfortable.

But there's a deeper kind of comfort. That's the comfort that comes in the middle of loss, injustice, and pain. The comfort that comes when we are especially uncomfortable. That kind of comfort can only come from beyond our circumstances and experiences. It comes from the God of all comfort, the one who showers us with comfort through Christ.

When we have no one on earth or heaven, we have him.

"God of comfort, may we rely on you alone."

JANUARY
14

HYMN

Savior, Savior, / Hear my humble cry; / While on others Thou art calling, / Do not pass me by

SCRIPTURE

Humble yourselves before the Lord, and he will lift you up in honor (James 4:10).

MEDITATION

What does it take to ensure that Jesus, the gentle Savior, will not pass us by?

It takes humility.

Humility is not putting ourselves down. It's seeing ourselves for who we truly are. We are blind like Bartimaeus. We are frantic parents who cannot completely protect our children. We are surrounded by challenges that are beyond our abilities. We need to shout for a Savior.

And what a Savior we have! He heals! He casts out our demons! He comforts! What he asks from us is to rely on him daily. If we look for him this day, he will not pass us by.

"Loving Savior, may we see ourselves for what we are—your beloved children."

JANUARY
15

HYMN

Holy, holy, holy is the Lord!

Sing, O ye people, gladly adore Him;

Let the mountains tremble at His word;

Let the hills be joyful before Him;

Mighty in wisdom, boundless in mercy,

Great is Jehovah, King over all.

SCRIPTURE

Let the hills sing out their songs of joy (Psalm 98:8).

MEDITATION

"Holy" seems like such an abstract word. But here in this hymn and in many places in the Bible, holy is a word of amazing power. The holiness of the Lord moves mountains, echoes joyfully through the hills, and causes God's people to sing.

What does it mean to be holy? It's hard for many to hear that word without thinking of hypocritical judgmentalism. But holy is the word the Bible uses to describe the very character of God. All descriptions of God—Almighty, Love, King, Father, Mother, Creator, Friend, Beauty, Goodness, beyond imagination—can be summarized by this, "Holy, Holy, Holy, is the Lord."

"Holy Lord, may we gladly adore you this day."

JANUARY 16

HYMN

Praise Him, praise Him! shout aloud for joy,

Watchman of Zion, herald the story;

Sin and death His kingdom shall destroy;

All the earth shall sing of His glory;

Praise Him, ye angels, ye who behold Him,

Robed in His splendor, matchless, divine.

SCRIPTURE

Let all that I am praise the Lord. O Lord my God, how great you are! You are robed with honor and majesty (Psalm 104:1).

MEDITATION

We Americans got rid of our king more than two centuries ago, but we still like the spectacle of a coronation or royal wedding—uniforms, robes, and crowns.

God wraps himself in glory, honor, and majesty. This marvelous spectacle calls forth amazement and praise from the entire creation. The Lord does not ask us to praise him because he needs affirmation. Just as an awesome storm or a beautiful sunset evokes a reaction, we praise God because it is our natural response to his power, beauty, and glory.

"Holy One, may we catch a glimpse of your glory today."

JANUARY
17

HYMN

King eternal, blessed be His name!

So may His children gladly adore Him;

When in Heav'n we join the happy strain,

When we cast our bright crowns before Him;

There in His likeness joyful awaking,

There we shall see Him, there we shall sing.

SCRIPTURE

And they will see his face, and his name will be written on their foreheads (Revelation 22:4).

MEDITATION

We walk by faith, not by sight. We catch glimpses of God, but we must trust him especially when we cannot see. At times God seems completely absent. Or worse, he seems to be against us. "How can this happen?" we ask. "Where is God?"

We walk by faith, but sight is coming. We will see God face to face. The anticipation of this beautiful vision keeps us going when things are dark. The promise of seeing God must have meant so much to the blind Fanny Crosby. It means so much to us who are often blind to the ways of the Lord.

"God of light, hasten the day when we see you face to face."

JANUARY
18

HYMN

More like Jesus would I be, / let my Savior dwell with me; / Fill my soul with peace and love, / make me gentle as a dove;

SCRIPTURE

That is how we know we are living in him. Those who say they live in God should live their lives as Jesus did (I John 2:5-6).

MEDITATION

Do you remember when you first learned to write? A parent or a teacher would show you how to write each letter. Then you would laboriously follow their example, making errors with every letter. But soon you could write. And now you write without thinking of how to make each letter.

Imitation is hard. Learning takes time. So it is with following Jesus. Each day we slowly, sometimes painfully, follow his example. The verse from the hymn speaks particularly of that slow, methodical learning of peace, love, and gentleness. Our teacher is here, patiently showing us the way. He knows learning takes time. His name is Jesus.

"Teacher, gently shape us into your image of peace and love."

JANUARY
19

HYMN

More like Jesus, while I go, pilgrim in this world below; Poor in spirit would I be; let my Savior dwell in me.

SCRIPTURE

Dear friends, I warn you as "temporary residents and foreigners" to keep away from worldly desires that wage war against your very souls (1 Peter 2:11).

MEDITATION

Do you sometimes feel like a stranger in your own land? More like a tourist than someone who grew up here? Thoughtful Christians still do not feel at home in this world. We work in the world. We even fit in to some extent. But at times it is clear that we are strangers. We get lost in a world whose roads are different than ours. At times we don't speak the language of our culture. It is foreign to us. We repeatedly face homelessness here. We do not value what others value so they shun and ignore us. We get strange looks and hear whispers behind our back. We are temporary residents, pilgrims passing through.

Jesus felt the same way. Homeless here, we are at home with him.

"Jesus, may I join you in your pilgrimage today."

JANUARY
20

HYMN

If He hears the raven's cry, / if His ever watchful eye / Marks the sparrows when they fall, / surely He will hear my call.

SCRIPTURE

What is the price of two sparrows—one copper coin? But not a single sparrow can fall to the ground without your Father knowing it (Matthew 10:29).

MEDITATION

I spend a lot of time watching birds. I'm amazed by their variety, their beauty, and their habits. There are over fifty billion birds on earth. The loss of a single one cannot count for much.

Yet we serve a Creator who not only made the world but who cares for every creature in it. When I'm in a place crowded with people, I sometimes wonder about their stories. And I wonder how God can keep track of all of them. But he does, all eight billion of them. He knows them all by name, knows the number of hairs on their heads, knows their hopes and fears.

So we should not be afraid. He always hears our call.

"Creator God, mark me when I fall today."

JANUARY 21

HYMN

He will teach me how to live, / all my sinful thoughts forgive;

Pure in heart I still would be, / let my Savior dwell in me.

SCRIPTURE

God blesses those whose hearts are pure, for they will see God (Matthew 5:8).

MEDITATION

We treasure pure water. Many of us buy it in bottles or spend on water purifiers in our homes. Pure water means nothing but water. No dirt, no contamination, no bad taste.

But what does it mean to be pure in heart?

Soren Kierkegaard said, "Purity of heart is to will one thing." That is, our heart, our will, is focused only on God. We concentrate only on the good. We do not desire God and something else. We do not obey God so he will give us health or happiness or comfort or even forgiveness. Like Jesus, we serve God because he is God. "Not my will but yours be done."

So this day, in all that we do, may our focus be on God alone. Let us will one thing—that God's will be done in us. And this we can do because our Savior dwells in us.

"Not my will, but yours be done."

JANUARY
22

HYMN

More like Jesus when I pray, May I rest me by His side,

more like Jesus day by day, where the tranquil waters glide.

SCRIPTURE

Once Jesus was in a certain place praying. As he finished, one of his disciples came to him and said, "Lord, teach us to pray, just as John taught his disciples" (Luke 11:1).

MEDITATION

Like many Christians, I pray the Lord's prayer daily. Most days I pray the prayer several times.

That comes with a challenge to mean the prayer each time I say it. I sometimes find myself in the middle of the prayer and realize I am not thinking of the words I say. Because I say it so often, I sometimes rush through it.

So I ask the Lord to slow down my prayer. I speak each word slowly, sometimes out loud. I sometimes even read the prayer in a language other than English (my first language) in order to make the words new to me. I don't think these are magic words, but when the disciples ask for instruction in prayer, Jesus gave these precious words. So we can be like Jesus as we pray.

"Lord Jesus, thank you for the 'Our Father…'"

JANUARY
23

HYMN

Born of Him through grace renewed,

by His love my will subdued,

Rich in faith I still would be,

let my Savior dwell in me.

SCRIPTURE

Jesus replied, "All who love me will do what I say. My Father will love them, and we will come and make our home with each of them." (John 14:23).

MEDITATION

We should be more like Jesus. That's a tall order. It is beyond our ability, no matter how hard we try, to be like the sinless Son of God. Trying harder to be so only leads to frustration and guilt.

The Bible makes it clear that Jesus is our example. The good news is that we can be like him because we are him. Or rather he is in us. Through the Holy Spirit, Father and Son make their home in us. Our relationship with Jesus is therefore more personal and powerful than following his example, as we would follow the example of any good leader.

"Savior, today may I let you dwell in me."

JANUARY
24

HYMN

Slow to anger, full of kindness,   Wash me in Thy healing fountain,

Rich in mercy, Lord, Thou art,   Take away my sinful heart.

SCRIPTURE

On that day a fountain will be opened for the dynasty of David and for the people of Jerusalem, a fountain to cleanse them from all their sins and impurity (Zechariah 13:1).

MEDITATION

After a hard day of manual labor or even after an hour of piddling in the garden, it feels great to have a shower and feel clean.

I remember vividly that sense of cleanness I felt when I was baptized. I was young but had been told repeatedly what a sinner I was. And now my sins were washed away.

You might or might not have similar memories, but we all know the thrill of cleansing, the joy of a fresh start. That happens not only at our baptisms, but if we continue to journey with Jesus, it happens each day. Jesus washes us clean each day and each moment. He constantly gives us pure hearts. All he asks is for us to trust his kindness and mercy.

"Lord, wash me clean this day. Create in me a pure heart."

JANUARY 25

HYMN

Thou wilt never, never leave me,   Teach, O teach me how to praise Thee,

If I give myself to Thee,   Tell me what my life should be.

SCRIPTURE

For God has said, "I will never fail you. I will never abandon you" (Hebrews 13:5).

MEDITATION

One of my most vivid childhood memories is being lost in a store. I was with my mother and got distracted by something. The next thing I knew, I looked up and Mom was gone! I was alone. I thought she'd never return.

Of course, Mom was in the next aisle and immediately returned to comfort me. But that was not the last time I felt abandoned.

Have you ever felt abandoned by God? You are not alone. All who follow Jesus sometimes feel abandoned. "I relied on God, and he left me on my own." "Why doesn't God do something?" Jesus felt abandoned too. "My God, My God, why have you forsaken me?"

But God did not abandon his beloved Son. He raised him from the dead. And he will never abandon us as his beloved children. He's in the next aisle. Just wait for his comfort.

"Father, may we continue to look for you when we feel abandoned."

JANUARY
26

HYMN

May Thy ever gracious Spirit,

Lead me in the way of truth,

May I learn the voice of wisdom,

In the early days of youth.

SCRIPTURE

And I will ask the Father, and he will give you another Advocate, who will never leave you. He is the Holy Spirit, who leads into all truth (John 14:16-17).

MEDITATION

Truth has fallen on tough times. Some deny that there is no truth except what is "true for me." Others are sure they have the truth and are ready to fight and destroy anyone who threatens it.

Where do we find the deepest truths, the truths about ourselves, others, the world, and God? Certainly, in the God-breathed Scriptures. But we have more than that. We have the One who is embodied truth—Jesus. Yet those who had been with Jesus for years needed more truth.

Jesus promises the Spirit who lives inside us and leads to all truth. That does not mean we have all the answers. Instead, the Spirit calls us not to the pride of those who know they have the truth, but to the humility of those who are constantly listening to the Spirit.

"In youth or old age, may we hear the wisdom of the Spirit."

JANUARY
27

HYMN

O! how sweet to rest confiding,
On Thy Word that cannot fail,
Strong in Thee, whate'er my trials,
Through Thy grace I must prevail.

SCRIPTURE

For the word of God will never fail (Luke 1:37).

MEDITATION

God speaks! What a comforting thought. We care not left alone without a word from God, stumbling through life with only human words to guide us.

God speaks! He spoke the world into existence. "Let there be…"

God speaks! He spoke to Abraham. He spoke to Moses and his people at Sinai. He spoke through judges and kings and prophets. "Thus says the Lord…"

God speaks! He speaks through Scripture. "All scripture is God-breathed…"

God speaks! He speaks in Jesus. "And the Word became flesh."

God speaks! And we can rest in the certainty of his word. "For God so loved…"

God speaks! Are we listening?

"Word of God, come into my heart today and bring me rest, strength, and grace."

JANUARY
28

HYMN

I would go the pilgrim's journey,
Onward to the promised land;
I would reach the golden city,
There to join the angel band.

SCRIPTURE

I was glad when they said to me, "Let us go to the house of the Lord" (Psalm 122:1).

MEDITATION

I love to travel. Planning the trip is almost as fun as the trip itself. Looking at guidebooks, designing the daily itinerary, and imagining the sights—all bring me extraordinary joy.

The trips themselves are a mixed blessing. Things never go as planned. Distances are longer on the ground than on maps. I find myself more tired than I expected. The language and the food and the culture are strange. Yet I so much enjoy seeing the world.

But no matter how long or short the trip is, it's always a thrill to come home. Home to the familiar and comfortable. Home to family (the same root word as familiar).

We are but travelers in this life. Tourists. Pilgrims. The way in this strange country is often hard. The golden city, the promised land awaits. Home. It's always a joy to come home.

"Jesus, be our guide on this pilgrimage, then bring us home."

JANUARY 29

HYMN

Heavenly Father, we beseech Thee,
Grant Thy blessing ere we part;
Take us in Thy care and keeping,
Guard from evil every heart.

SCRIPTURE

Then you will experience God's peace, which exceeds anything we can understand. His peace will guard your hearts and minds as you live in Christ Jesus (Philippians 4:7).

MEDITATION

We live in an age obsessed with security. Ads bombard us with frightening videos of intruders prepared to rob us or do worse to us. Only by subscribing to the home security system can we be safe.

We want our houses guarded, but who will guard our hearts? It's the inward fears that lead us to turn our homes into fortresses. Fear that we will be harmed. Fear that we don't measure up. Fear from the evils without and within.

God alone is the fortress of our hearts. He protects us from sin, from worry, and from all forms of trouble. Oh yes, the troubles come, but he gives the peace beyond our understanding.

"Father, bless us, keep us, guard us."

JANUARY
30

HYMN

Loving Savior, go Thou with us, / Be our Comfort and our Stay;

Grateful praise to Thee we render / For the joy we feel today.

SCRIPTURE

When doubts filled my mind, your comfort gave me renewed hope and cheer (Psalm 94:19).

MEDITATION

We Christians are sometimes criticized for ignoring evil. We just put on a happy face and pretend that the world is fine even though millions suffer oppression. There is sometimes truth in this criticism. Some offer "thoughts and prayers" when action is called for.

But this can be a false judgment of Christians. What many do not understand is that Jesus gives joy in the deepest of our miseries. It's not that we ignore evil. It's not that we enjoy pain. It's not that we are comfortable and ignore the exploitation of others.

It is a trust in a Savior who suffers with us. Trust that he has made and will make things right. Trust in his comfort and security. That trust allows us to see the beauty that surrounds us, even when the ugly intrudes.

Such trust leads to praise for the joy we feel today.

"Loving Savior, go with us in joy today."

JANUARY 31

HYMN

Holy Spirit, dwell within us, May we tread the path to glory,

May our souls Thy temple be; Led and guided still by Thee.

SCRIPTURE

We are carefully joined together in him, becoming a holy temple for the Lord. Through him you Gentiles are also being made part of this dwelling where God lives by his Spirit (Ephesians 2:21-22).

MEDITATION

I have often stood in awe at great cathedrals. Their soaring heights move my soul to soar with them. The wonders of stained glass, carved stone, and gilded monuments tell the stories of saints of old.

We are a cathedral, a temple to the Lord. Not only is it that each of us houses Father, Son, and Spirit, but together we are being built into a house for God.

When we look at ourselves and at those who sit beside us as we worship, it may not look like much of a cathedral. But if we could see each other through God's eyes, the eyes of the one who loves us infinitely, we could see the most magnificent temple of the Holy Spirit.

"God, give us eyes to see others the way you see them, as sanctuaries for your presence."

FEBRUARY 1

HYMN

Heavenly Father, loving Savior, As among Thy saints and angels,

Holy Spirit, Three in One, So on earth Thy will be done.

SCRIPTURE

May the grace of the Lord Jesus Christ, the love of God, and the fellowship of the Holy Spirit be with you all (2 Corinthians 13:14).

MEDITATION

The very essence of God is relationship—Father, Son, and Spirit. The name for that relationship is love. God is love, and he draws us into that eternal dance of Father, Son, and Spirit.

That is why Jesus taught us to pray, "Your will be done on earth as in heaven." The heavenly beings do God's will immediately and joyfully because those beings spring from the creative relationship of the Trinity. We and our world were spoken into creation from the same loving bond.

Yet we are a part of a fallen world. Jesus came to make our relationship with God and our fellow creatures whole again. So we journey into the very heart of God.

"Lord, hasten the day when your will is done completely by all creation."

FEBRUARY 2

HYMN

Awake! for the trumpet is sounding!

Awake to its call, and obey!

The voice of our Leader cries, "Onward!"

Oh, let us no longer delay!

SCRIPTURE

This is all the more urgent, for you know how late it is; time is running out. Wake up, for our salvation is nearer now than when we first believed (Romans 13:11).

MEDITATION

"Wake up!"

These are words I often do not like to hear. In the middle of sweet sleep, these words sound abrupt and irritating.

They are particularly irritating when someone says them to us when we are not asleep. "Wake up!" Those who love us sometimes say these words when we are not paying attention to the world around us. We sometimes sleepwalk through life and need a wake-up call.

So our loving Savior says, "Wake up! Pay attention! Salvation is near! Follow me!" He says this though Scripture, through others who care for us, and through difficult situations. He sounds reveille in our sleeping ears, saying "battle stations."

"Commanding leader, wake us up to follow you into battle."

FEBRUARY
3

HYMN

No truce while the foe is unconquered;

No laying the armor down!

No peace till the battle is ended,

And victory wins the crown!

SCRIPTURE

For we are not fighting against flesh-and-blood enemies, but against evil rulers and authorities of the unseen world, against mighty powers in this dark world, and against evil spirits in the heavenly places (Ephesians 6:12).

MEDITATION

Battle imagery is found throughout the Bible. The Lord gives his people victory. We must courageously enter the battle in his name. The foes of the Lord must be vanquished!

Such imagery bothers me. God is a God of love. Jesus is the Prince of peace. We have a Spirit of joy. Why all the battle and killing language? This especially bothers me in an age where we demonize our political opponents, seeing no good in them. Or we dehumanize our nation's enemies so we might in good conscience destroy them.

We must remember that other people are not our enemies. Or, if we think them so, Jesus says we must love them. But we do have an enemy. And we are in a cosmic battle.

"Lord of heaven's armies, fight for us today."

FEBRUARY

4

HYMN

Then gird on the sword of the Spirit,

With helmet, and breastplate, and shield;

And valiantly follow your captain,

Determined you never will yield!

SCRIPTURE

Put on salvation as your helmet, and take the sword of the Spirit, which is the word of God (Ephesians 6:17).

MEDITATION

One cannot escape the language of war. Not only is it throughout the Bible but it permeates almost every novel, play, and film. War language reflects the nature of reality—the constant struggle of good vs evil.

Therefore as followers of the Jesus who is both Prince of Peace (Isaiah 9:6) and the one who wages war (Revelation 19:11), we follow him into battle.

But look at our weapons—truth, righteousness, peace, faith, salvation, prayer, the Spirit, and the word of God (Ephesians 6:13-18). These are not weapons of violence but weapons of reconciliation. We defeat our enemies by loving them. That kind of love demands more courage, valor, and determination than the most horrendous and bloody battle ever fought.

"Lord Jesus, you gave your life for your enemies! Give us courage to fight that way."

FEBRUARY

5

HYMN

Then forward! O army of Zion, / With hearts that are loyal and brave! / Stand firm by the cross and its banner; / And rest in the "Mighty to save"!

SCRIPTURE

Stand your ground, putting on the belt of truth and the body armor of God's righteousness (Ephesians 6:14).

MEDITATION

Keep fighting. That's what Jesus did. In my struggle against temptation, I often give in quickly. Jesus experienced temptations greater than mine, greater because he continued to fight them. He was without sin only because at every fork of the road, he took the path of his Father, no matter how hard it was, even when it leads to the cross.

Keep fighting. That's what Jesus did. In our battles against injustice, we often give in quickly. "That's just the way it is," we say. "That's the best we can hope for." But Jesus will not settle until every wrong against the oppressed is made right.

Keep fighting. That's what Jesus leads us to do, even when it leads to our cross.

"Lord Jesus, may we stand firm in your cross today."

FEBRUARY 6

HYMN

Blessed Redeemer, full of compassion,

Great is Thy mercy, boundless and free;

Now in my weakness, seeking Thy favor,

Lord, I am coming closer to Thee.

SCRIPTURE

When he saw the crowds, he had compassion on them because they were confused and helpless, like sheep without a shepherd (Matthew 9:36)

MEDITATION

It's sometimes hard to admit we need help. We've been taught to be self-reliant. Accepting charity is a shameful thing.

Yet when we stand before God, we can only ask for help. And we ask knowing that we do not deserve it. We have not done all that we can do. Even if we think we've done our best, we find our best is not enough. We need help!

Jesus gives us whatever help we need. He does this strictly out of his boundless compassion. Accepting his charity is not a shameful thing, but an honor. But to receive his compassionate help we must draw closer to him. We must trust his goodness and his power to help us, no matter what we face.

"Lord, come to our assistance. Make haste to help us."

FEBRUARY 7

HYMN

Blessed Redeemer, Thou art my refuge,

Under Thy watch-care, safe I shall be;

Gladly adoring, joyfully trusting,

Still I am coming closer to Thee.

SCRIPTURE

Therefore, we who have fled to him for refuge can have great confidence as we hold to the hope that lies before us (Hebrews 6:18).

MEDITATION

Perhaps you have a retreat, a refuge. A place where you can get away from all that bothers you. That's the theory behind most vacations and holidays.

But what if you needed a genuine refuge? What if war or persecution or famine made it necessary for you to flee your home? What if you were a refugee?

For many of us, that's hard to imagine. But there are people in our towns and neighborhoods who don't have to imagine. They may have been doctors or lawyers or leaders in their country but now they clean our houses and mow our grass to put food on the table.

Spiritually we are all refugees. We have no power and no home. We fled one home and look for another, better one. We have not arrived but are on a journey.

"Jesus, be our refuge this day. You are our place of safety and joy."

FEBRUARY

8

HYMN

Blessed Redeemer, gracious and tender,

Now and forever dwell Thou in me;

Thou, my protector, shield and defender,

Draw me and keep me closer to Thee.

SCRIPTURE

Because of God's tender mercy, the morning light from heaven is about to break upon us (Luke 1:78).

MEDITATION

Tender. Softhearted. Bighearted. Warmhearted.

Our God has a tender heart. His power is beyond our imagination, yet he treats us with gentleness and kindness.

The Bible uses many word pictures to speak of this tenderhearted God. God is a shepherd who puts the lost sheep on his shoulder. God is the gardener who carefully tends his plants. God is the hen who protects her chicks under her wings. God is the physician who touches and heals. God is the teacher, patient with his students, and a father who waits for the lost boy. God is the mother who nurses her newborn child.

God—Father, Son, Spirit—is gracious and tender.

"Gracious and Tender Redeemer, be gentle with us this day."

FEBRUARY 9

HYMN

Blessed Redeemer, wonderful Savior,

Fountain of wisdom, Ancient of Days,

Hope of the faithful, light of all ages,

Jesus my Savior, Thee will I praise.

SCRIPTURE

Are any of you suffering hardships? You should pray. Are any of you happy? You should sing praises (James 5:13).

MEDITATION

Why does God demand praise? When humans demand praise, we rightly see them as either egotistic or with low self-esteem. Does God need our praise?

No. He wants our praise because he wants us. When we have a relationship with God, we think of God, experience God, and see God, unclearly to be sure, but still we see.

When we see God, we cannot help but praise. It's similar to our reaction to a splendid sunset, a charming newborn, or a stunning flower. We smile. Something within us bursts forth with joy. We are caught up in something greater than ourselves. Captured by beauty.

So it is when we see the One who is Redeemer, Savior, Wisdom, Hope, and Light.

"God of Beauty, Jesus our Savior, Spirit of Life, may we praise you this day."

FEBRUARY
10

HYMN

The Lord in Zion reigneth, let all the world rejoice, And come before His throne of grace with tuneful heart and voice;

The Lord in Zion reigneth, and there His praise shall ring, To Him shall princes bend the knee and kings their glory bring.

SCRIPTURE

Let the heavens be glad, and the earth rejoice! Tell all the nations, "The Lord reigns!" (1 Chronicles 16:31).

MEDITATION

Who rules the world?

Presidents, Prime Ministers, and kings rule the world. They seem to have all the power. They make decisions that affect the welfare of billions of people.

Billionaires and corporations rule the world. No matter what country you visit, you see their names on buildings, billboards, and products. Their decisions affect everyone on earth.

The media rules the world. They tell us what is "true." They tell us what politician to support and what corporations should get our money. Everyone listens to them.

By contrast, we believe the Lord reigns over every prince.

"Lord, open our eyes to your reign over our world."

FEBRUARY 11

HYMN

The Lord in Zion reigneth, and who so great as He? The depths of earth are in His hands; He rules the mighty sea.

O crown His name with honor, and let His standard wave, Till distant isles beyond the deep shall own His power to save.

SCRIPTURE

You rule the oceans. You subdue their storm-tossed waves (Psalm 89:9).

MEDITATION

I've always liked the romance of the sea but not the reality. I did not grow up with boats. I don't know firsthand about sailing on the sea.

Those who do know firsthand, whether weekend sailors or professional fishermen, have great respect for the power of the ocean. They know the weather can change in an instant. They know the destruction and loss of life a storm can bring. The Israelites were not much of a sea-faring people. The sea represented chaos, not a charming day at the beach.

God's people know the chaos that surrounds our lives. The sea of change catches us off guard and we don't know what to do. Helpless, we cry out in the storms of life. The One who rules the seas hears us.

"Ruler of the sea, calm the chaos of our lives this day."

FEBRUARY

12

HYMN

The Lord in Zion reigneth, these hours to Him belong; O enter now His temple gates, and fill His courts with song; Beneath His royal banner let every creature fall, Exalt the King of heaven and earth, and crown Him Lord of all.

SCRIPTURE

Enter his gates with thanksgiving; go into his courts with praise. Give thanks to him and praise his name (Psalm 100:4).

MEDITATION

Are there places in our lives that we think belong to us, not to God?

Of course, God cares about our spiritual life, our time at church or at prayer. He wants us to have a religious life. But what about business? Doesn't it operate on different rules? Or politics, or our leisure time, or how we invest? Aren't those up to us?

The Lord reigns. He rules every part of our life. He doesn't care about our "spiritual life," he wants every moment of every day. What happens when we surrender our whole life to the Lord, even those parts we think belong to us? What happens when we crown him Lord of all?

Joy. We enter his presence with song.

"Almighty God, rule my life completely this day, that I may sing your praises."

FEBRUARY 13

HYMN

Tell me the story of Jesus,

Write on my heart every word.

Tell me the story most precious,

Sweetest that ever was heard.

SCRIPTURE

So beginning with this same Scripture, Philip told him the Good News about Jesus (Acts 8:35).

MEDITATION

"Mama, tell me a story!" That's what I said as a kid. And so Mama did. Usually, it was a Bible story, and most often a story of Jesus.

I'm so glad my parents told me the story of Jesus. Perhaps your parents did too. Or perhaps you came to the story of Jesus later in life. For those who have always known the story there is a particular danger. We might take the story for granted. It becomes an old hat—worn out, out of date, and overly familiar. It's the same old "Jesus, Jesus, Jesus."

But whether the story is old or newer to us, it's a story we need to hear again with new ears. It is the most precious, sweetest story. The story of a God who so loved us that he became one of us.

"Open the ears of our hearts to hear the story of Jesus anew."

FEBRUARY
14

HYMN

Tell how the angels in chorus,   "Glory to God in the highest!

Sang as they welcomed His birth.   Peace and good tidings to earth."

SCRIPTURE

Suddenly, the angel was joined by a vast host of others —the armies of heaven—praising God and saying, "Glory to God in highest heaven, and peace on earth to those with whom God is pleased" (Luke 2:13-14).

MEDITATION

Peace. It would be a wonderful thing to have peace. But all we see and hear in the media is conflict. There is news of war every day—bombings, atrocities, and the targeting of innocents. There are battles over moral issues, clashes between political parties, and ethnic strife. Shootings, stabbings, beatings, and muggings.

It's been over two thousand years since the angels sang of peace. When will it come?

It already has. It came in the birth of a baby in Bethlehem. Yes, conflicts still remain, but they will not last forever. Soon every knee will bow before this child, and there will be peace in the new heavens and earth.

"Prince of peace, rule in our hearts and our world today."

FEBRUARY
15

HYMN

Fasting alone in the desert,
Tell of the days that are past.
How for our sins He was tempted,
Yet was triumphant at last.

SCRIPTURE

Then Jesus was led by the Spirit into the wilderness to be tempted there by the devil. For forty days and forty nights he fasted and became very hungry (Matthew 4:1-2).

MEDITATION

Days pass by quickly. Unless you are fasting. Then time crawls until all you can think about is endurance. "Just get me through this," you pray. But through the endurance comes the experience of the presence of God.

Temptation also comes. "Eat this and your hunger will stop." But God alone satisfies. "If God loves you, he will protect you." Yes, but we do not test or control our God. "You can rule the world and make it better." Yes, but only through obedience.

The Spirit leads us into the desert to make us stronger, strong enough to resist the voices of the world that promise much but do not deliver. Strong enough to hear one voice.

"Lord Jesus, fast with us so we might hear only the word from God."

FEBRUARY
16

HYMN

Tell of the years of His labor,   He was despised and afflicted,

Tell of the sorrow He bore.   Homeless, rejected and poor.

SCRIPTURE

You know the generous grace of our Lord Jesus Christ. Though he was rich, yet for your sakes he became poor, so that by his poverty he could make you rich (2 Corinthians 8:9).

MEDITATION

I was born two generations from poverty. My grandparents at one point lived in a tarpaper shack with no inside plumbing. Through no fault of my own, I was born into a comfortable middle-class family (what much of the world would call rich). I was taught to give an honest day's work for an honest day's pay so I would not have to depend on others.

As a carpenter, Jesus knew the value of hard work. If you read the Gospels, you find that he worked long days in his ministry—teaching, walking, and healing.

Jesus chose to be poor. Of course, the problem with poor people is that they depend on others. So Jesus depended on a group of generous women to provide for him and his disciples (Luke 8:1-3). Why did he choose to depend on others? So he could teach us to depend on God.

"Generous God, remind us that we depend on you for daily bread."

FEBRUARY 17

HYMN

Tell of the cross where they nailed Him,
Writhing in anguish and pain.

Tell of the grave where they laid Him,
Tell how He liveth again.

SCRIPTURE

I passed on to you what was most important and what had also been passed on to me. Christ died for our sins, just as the Scriptures said. He was buried, and he was raised from the dead on the third day, just as the Scriptures said (1 Corinthians 15:3-4).

MEDITATION

It is crucial to meditate on the pains Jesus suffered on the cross, including the pain of shame and the pain of carrying our sins. But the resurrection changes the meaning of the cross. Without the resurrection, the cross is only about pain, shame, and injustice. In light of the resurrection, the cross becomes a symbol of dying and undying love. Jesus has his hands nailed widespread in welcome to all who will come to him. His crown of thorns becomes a garland of victory. His spilled blood is not about death, but eternal life. His last words, "Father, I entrust my spirit into your hands!" (Luke 23:46), become not last words, but words that summarize a life of trust. He lives again. That changes everything.

"Lord Jesus, may I see the cross this day through the lens of resurrection."

FEBRUARY
18

HYMN

Love in that story so tender,

Clearer than ever I see.

Stay, let me weep while you whisper,

Love paid the ransom for me.

SCRIPTURE

Rise up! Help us! Ransom us because of your unfailing love (Psalm 44:26).

MEDITATION

It's the plot of countless television shows. Someone is kidnapped and a ransom must be paid.

The ransom language is used of the death of Jesus (Mark 10:45, 1 Peter 1:18-20, Revelation 5:9). To whom was the ransom paid? Some suggest to God, others to Satan or to death. It may seem strange for God the Father to demand a ransom for us, but if you think of fallen humanity under the curse of death, then perhaps that makes sense.

The crucial point is that God paid the ransom for us in the death of Jesus, the Son of God. Love paid the ransom for me and for you. We weep at the cross, not just because of the pain and shame we witness, but because of the awareness of the depths of God's love. Our tears are tears of those beloved by God. They are tears of joy.

"Lord Jesus, may we be overwhelmed by the power of your love."

FEBRUARY 19

HYMN

Be strong and courageous whate'er may befall, We know our Redeemer will answer our call; Tho' sorrow and trials are weighing us down, Yet hope looks away from the cross to the crown.

SCRIPTURE

And now the prize awaits me—the crown of righteousness, which the Lord, the righteous Judge, will give me on the day of his return. And the prize is not just for me but for all who eagerly look forward to his appearing (2 Timothy 4:8).

MEDITATION

The crown promised to the faithful does not refer to the royal crown with gold and jewels but to the wreath of laurel leaves placed on the head of those who won athletic contests.

Everyone loves a winner. Everyone wants to win. The promise we have is that we will be victorious. But the contest will be hard fought. Victory does not come easily. Sorrows and trials weigh us down. The path to triumph always goes through the cross.

We fool ourselves when we think God promises an easy life. Jesus did not have one. Neither will his followers. But the gold medal awaits those who finish.

"Lord Jesus, may we look forward to the day of your return, the day of victory."

FEBRUARY
20

HYMN

His cup of affliction was filled to the brim,

And are we not willing to suffer for Him?

The robe of His glory for us He laid down,

To show us the path from the cross to the crown.

SCRIPTURE

"Oh yes," they replied, "we are able!" Then Jesus told them, "You will indeed drink from my bitter cup and be baptized with my baptism of suffering" (Mark 10:39).

MEDITATION

Following Jesus should be easy. At least, like James and John in the verse above, we think it should be easy. Jesus is the King who will win the victory. All we have to do is follow him and we will win.

But Jesus wins by losing. The path to glory always goes through the cross. Therefore following him always means a bitter cup and a painful baptism.

It's been comfortable for me to follow Jesus. Perhaps if I truly follow, I will have to suffer for the sake of others. I must learn to lose so I can win.

"Lord Jesus, give us strength to drink your cup and suffer your baptism!"

FEBRUARY
21

HYMN

This life is a conflict, a battle with sin,

Yet trusting in Jesus thro' grace we shall win;

The world may oppose us, the tempter may frown, Yet faith leadeth on from the cross to the crown.

SCRIPTURE

After all, you have not yet given your lives in your struggle against sin (Hebrews 12:4).

MEDITATION

Martyrdom.

It seems so strange to most of us. Yes, we know that many of the early Christians gave their lives for their faith. Yes, we have heard accounts of contemporary martyrs for Christ in other countries. But those stories seem far removed from us in time or in distance.

We've had it pretty easy as Christians.

Yet, when Jesus demands we take up the cross daily, he is not calling all his followers to literally die for him. He is calling all of us to fight the daily battle against sin and discouragement. He is promising that some will oppose us. He is insisting that we do not give up the fight, but that we daily trust in him.

"Jesus, Savior, give us strength to fight and die for one more day."

FEBRUARY
22

HYMN

Tho' friends that are dearest have gone from our sight,

'Tis only to enter the mansions of light;

Their warfare is over, their burdens laid down, How short was their path from the cross to the crown!

SCRIPTURE

For to me, living means living for Christ, and dying is even better (Philippians 1:21).

MEDITATION

The world would have us believe that this life is the whole of our existence: "Life is short and then you die." What a depressing thought!

But we believe that was not the whole story of Jesus. His life was short. He died. But we believe he rose from the dead, ascended to heaven, and is at the right hand of the Father in glory.

And we believe that those we love, although their lives were short and they died, have gone to be with the Lord, awaiting his return and their resurrection.

So even though following Jesus brings trouble and calls us to die with him, death is not the end of our relationship with God or with others. The path goes through the cross, but it ends in glory.

"Lord Jesus, strengthen our trust in your resurrection and in our own."

FEBRUARY 23

HYMN

From the cross to the crown let us follow our Lord, From the cross to the crown let us cling to His Word; Tho' sorrow and trials are weighing us down, Yet faith leads us on from the cross to the crown!

SCRIPTURE

Then Jesus said to his disciples, "If any of you wants to be my follower, you must give up your own way, take up your cross, and follow me" (Matthew 16:24).

MEDITATION

So the question is, "Do we believe what Jesus said?"

He said, "Don't let your hearts be troubled. Trust in God, and trust also in me. There is more than enough room in my Father's home. If this were not so would I have told you that I am going to prepare a place for you? When everything is ready, I will come and get you, so that you will always be with me where I am" (John 14:1-3).

If we cling to those words from Jesus, we can endure our sorrows and trials. When we stand at the grave of the one we love, we can believe that death is not final, although it looks that way. When we contemplate our own cross and death, we can still confidently follow our Lord.

"Savior, may we cling to your word."

FEBRUARY
24

HYMN

There's a friend that abides evermore, And that friend is the Lord, my king; Of the peace I received, When His Word I believed, In the fullness of joy I will sing.

SCRIPTURE

I no longer call you slaves, because a master doesn't confide in his slaves. Now you are my friends, since I have told you everything the Father told me (John 15:15).

MEDITATION

Everyone wants to have friends and to be a friend. Indeed, in our society, we may suffer from "friend inflation," in that we have so many people we call friends that we have devalued friendship. Where everyone is your friend, no one truly is.

We are called to be friends of God, called to a personal, intimate relationship with the Almighty. This is a call to action, not complacency. We must embrace the gift of God's friendship. We must be genuine friends to others. We must set the world on fire with the frightening, dangerous love of God that breaks down barriers and proclaims peace. In worship and service, we encounter a God who no longer calls us slaves, but friends, a Jesus who wants us to share in the self-giving love of the Father.

"Friend Jesus, thank you for giving us a relationship with the Almighty."

FEBRUARY 25

HYMN

There's a friend that abides evermore,

And I praise Him with loud acclaim;

For the life that is mine

Through His mercy divine;

Still I sing in my joy, "Bless His name!"

SCRIPTURE

So now we can rejoice in our wonderful new relationship with God because our Lord Jesus Christ has made us friends of God (Romans 5:11).

MEDITATION

Friendship with God through Christ is completed in mission. If we are friends of God, we must be friends of others. That spiritual friendship is one that does not seek to have our needs fulfilled in friendship, but rather proclaims the reign of God over all. It is a dangerous love that opens us and our friends to the socially disruptive possibilities of the life of God.

Friendship with God and with one another may sound clannish and separatist— "we are God's friends, and you are not." But we are friends of God for the sake of the world. To be truly God's friend means we must see the world through his eyes and lead the world to a hopeful vision of a God who brings justice to the oppressed. To be a friend of the One who "so loved the world" calls us to solidarity with the downtrodden, "the least of these," the ones Jesus came to heal, free, and save.

"Friend Jesus, make us friends to others."

FEBRUARY
26

HYMN

There's a love that is strong as the hills That encircle His throne above; How it speaks to my soul When the dark billows roll, And my heart sings for joy, "God is love!"

SCRIPTURE

But anyone who does not love does not know God, for God is love. God showed how much he loved us by sending his one and only Son into the world so that we might have eternal life through him (1 John 4:8-9).

MEDITATION

We know God because God is love. Where we see genuine love, there God is. And the greatest display of that measureless love of God is in Jesus Christ. That's why those who do not recognize Jesus do not know God. They have failed to see the depth of his love.

If we know God as love, then we live in faith, not fear. The one in us, the power of love, Love Himself, is stronger than the hatred in the world. Perfect love drives out fear—fear of the world and fear of punishment.

And when God's love shines through the dark billows, our hearts can only sing that God is love!

"God of love, open our hearts to your love so we may in turn love others."

FEBRUARY
27

HYMN

There's a friend that abides evermore, And a friend that I long to see;

O, the song that will break, When to rapture I wake, And in glory with Him I shall be!

SCRIPTURE

Because I am righteous, I will see you. When I awake, I will see you face to face and be satisfied (Psalm 17:15).

MEDITATION

What would it be like to see Jesus? We've all imagined what that would be like. Would he look like the illustrations in our Bibles? Would he look like the Jesus we have seen in movies? Or would his appearance, his words, and his manner all surprise us? He was from the East. He did not look like many North Americans. He was in every way an immigrant. God immigrated to our world. The Word that was in the beginning became flesh and lived with us (John 1:14).

If we are to truly follow this foreigner, this immigrant, then we must embrace all of God's people, particularly those who are foreign to us. In the face of our brothers and sisters of different colors, languages, and customs, we see the one who entered our world for us.

That is the friend we long to see!

"Lord Jesus, we long to see you in glory! May we see you this day in the stranger."

FEBRUARY
28

HYMN

O come, quickly come!   O come to that friend so true;

He is calling you today,

SCRIPTURE

As Jesus was walking along, he saw a man named Matthew sitting at his tax collector's booth. "Follow me and be my disciple," Jesus said to him. So Matthew got up and followed him (Matthew 9:9).

MEDITATION

Jesus, our friend, came to us. "The Word became flesh." God himself became one of us.

But now that he has come to us, he asks us in turn to come to him. The usual biblical word for this is "repentance." Unfortunately, for many, that word just means to straighten up and quit our evil ways.

Repentance means much more than that. It means we turn to Jesus. We follow him. Like Matthew and the earliest disciples, we leave all that we know, all that we have accomplished, and all that we have dreamed, all to follow Jesus alone.

The one we come to, the one we follow, will prove to be our greatest friend.

"Friend Jesus, give us strength to leave all and follow you."

FEBRUARY
29

HYMN

He will be your faithful guide,
More than all the world beside,
And remember He has died for you.

SCRIPTURE

For since our friendship with God was restored by the death of his Son while we were still his enemies, we will certainly be saved through the life of his Son (Romans 5:10).

MEDITATION

Did you ever lose a good friend?

Maybe the loss came from neglect. You failed to keep in touch. Maybe the loss was more dramatic and severe. You had a falling out. Harsh words were said on both sides.

Have you ever reconciled with a friend? Put the past behind? Forgave them and were forgiven by them? What an immense joy to be friends again.

We broke our friendship with God through rebellion and sin. It was all our fault. Yet we did not make the first step toward reconciliation. God did. And what a step! He became human and died for us! And now friend Jesus saves us by his life!

"God, we thank you for restoring our friendship."

MARCH 1

HYMN

When Jesus comes to reward His servants, Whether it be noon or night, Faithful to Him will He find us watching, With our lamps all trimmed and bright?

SCRIPTURE

"So you, too, must keep watch! For you do not know the day or hour of my return" (Matthew 25:13).

MEDITATION

No one knows precisely when Christ will return; no one but God himself. Since we do not know, we should be ready.

What does it mean to be ready? Should we try to live each moment of each day with the conscious thought, "The Lord may come today?" I don't think we can. I don't even think we should. But the thought should be there behind our conscious thoughts, informing all that we do.

Many of us know what it's like to wait for a child to be born. The anticipation of our child's birth affects all we do or say or think months before the birth. As time grows closer, we go about our normal business, but always in the back of our minds is "This might be the day." It's the same with the Lord's coming. We know it's soon; we don't know when.

"Lord Jesus, make us ready for your arrival."

MARCH 2

HYMN

If, at the dawn of the early morning,

He shall call us one by one,

When to the Lord we restore our talents, Will He answer thee "Well done"?

SCRIPTURE

"The master was full of praise. 'Well done, my good and faithful servant. You have been faithful in handling this small amount, so now I will give you many more responsibilities. Let's celebrate together!'" (Matthew 25:21).

MEDITATION

It's hard to see judgment as a sign of love, but that's what it is. God loves us so much that he takes our choices seriously. If we think God is a tyrant and we hide our talents, then God will respect that decision.

Our God is a God of grace. Jesus is the friend of sinners. But if we hypocritically insist that we have a relationship with God when we ignore what he has entrusted to us, we fool only ourselves. If we think we are serving Jesus when we neglect the least of his brothers and sisters, we have forfeited any right to our inheritance as children. Judgment means life is real and earnest.

"God of grace, may we hear your call and share what you have given us."

MARCH 3

HYMN

Have we been true to the trust He left us?

If in our hearts there is naught condemns us,

Do we seek to do our best?

We shall have a glorious rest.

SCRIPTURE

Dear friends, if we don't feel guilty, we can come to God with bold confidence. And we will receive from him whatever we ask because we obey him and do the things that please him. (1 John 3:21-22).

MEDITATION

What does it mean to be God's children? It means living righteous lives that avoid sin. It means the love of our brothers and sisters. Love is shown by acts of compassion.

The world conspires to convince us that we are not worthy to be called God's children. Voices outside us, sometimes from those who are closest to us, and voices inside our own heads repeatedly say, "Who are you kidding? You cannot be a child of God. You are too broken, too little, too sinful."

Those voices are wrong. We come to a God who pronounces us "Not guilty" and who calls us his beloved children. A God who promises a glorious rest with him.

"Gracious God, take away our guilt and make us bold in your Presence."

MARCH 4

HYMN

Blessed are those whom the Lord finds watching,

In His glory they shall share;

If He shall come at the dawn or midnight,

Will He find us watching there?

SCRIPTURE

You also must be ready all the time, for the Son of Man will come when least expected (Matthew 24:44).

MEDITATION

Jesus encourages us to be ready for his coming. We stay ready not by constantly asking, "Will it be today?" but by living a quiet and obedient life so that whenever he comes, we will be found faithful. We stay ready by doing. We stay ready by remembering his teachings, his miracles, and his life. By reflecting on the real Jesus, the one who astounded his contemporaries, we begin to recognize him. We see him in the lives of those around us, we hear his voice in the words of Scripture, we feel his presence with us in prayer, and we rely on his help when tempted. By following his steps, we are being transformed in his image. By walking with him, we are being prepared for that day when we shall see him face to face.

"Lord Jesus, come quickly."

MARCH 5

HYMN

O can we say we are ready, brother? Ready for the soul's bright home? Say, will He find you and me still watching, Waiting, waiting when the Lord shall come?

SCRIPTURE

And they speak of how you are looking forward to the coming of God's Son from heaven—Jesus, whom God raised from the dead. He is the one who has rescued us from the terrors of the coming judgment (1 Thessalonians 1:10).

MEDITATION

Waiting. Waiting is always hard. It's hard to wait on the coming of Jesus. It's been two thousand years! It's hard to wait for the eternal pleasures of being with the Lord, particularly when we must give up the pleasures of unrestrained sexuality. It's hard to resist the call to worldly ambition, but instead to live quiet lives of daily work.

But waiting is so much easier if it is anticipation. Waiting for Christmas as a child was hard but it was a different kind of waiting from waiting in the dentist's office. We wait for what is to come with joyful anticipation. We will greet our returning King in the air and live with him forever in a new heaven and a new earth.

"Jesus, make us ready for your return."

MARCH 6

HYMN

Come, Lord, and let Thy power
On each and all descend,
While gathered in Thy holy name,
Before Thy throne we bend.

SCRIPTURE

So the message about the Lord spread widely and had a powerful effect (Acts 19:20).

MEDITATION

We do not want to admit that life is beyond our control. We search for power. We buy the latest exercise equipment or the new miracle drug or wonder surgery to gain control of our health. We attend the hot success seminar or read the best-selling self-help book to master our inner potential. We want more money not because we are misers but because we think it gives us power over an uncertain economy.

God promises us power beyond our wildest imaginations. He sends it through a Savior sent from heaven. As we bow before him, we receive the Spirit of power.

This message about the Lord had a powerful effect in those who heard it in the first century. It still has that powerful effect in our time as we gather in the holy name of Jesus.

"Lord Jesus, may we trust in your power, not in the false power of the world."

MARCH 7

HYMN

Come, Lord, and let Thy power
Each thought of self remove;
And may we feel as ne'er before
Thy pure and perfect love.

SCRIPTURE

All praise to God, the Father of our Lord Jesus Christ, who has blessed us with every spiritual blessing in the heavenly realms because we are united with Christ (Ephesians 1:3).

MEDITATION

Can we do it?

Can we really let go of our deep-seated desire to control our own lives? Can we refuse the "magic" answers of our culture, all those things that promise safety, success, and happiness? Can we truly let go of the wheel and let God alone do the driving? What happens if we let God alone rule our destinies? What is it he will do to us?

He will bless beyond belief. God has blessed us (past tense) in the heavenly realms. In one sense, heaven is a reality to us now. We already experience life with the eternal God who lives in the heavens. While we live here on earth, by faith we also now live with Christ and in Christ in heaven. God is blessing us now as we feel his perfect love.

"God of power, bless us with your powerful love."

MARCH 8

HYMN

Our waiting, longing eyes,

Are looking up to Thee,

O may we, in Thy smiling face,

Our Father's glory see.

SCRIPTURE

I pray that your hearts will be flooded with light so that you can understand the confident hope he has given to those he called… (Ephesians 1:18).

MEDITATION

How do we get to know someone? We work together. We play together. We see them. We talk. We laugh. We cry. Yet in all of this, we can only know others if they let us. They must drop their guard, let down their masks, and reveal themselves to us. Knowing someone always comes as a gift.

It's the same way with God. How did we come to know God? There are many true answers. Our mamas taught us. We read our Bibles. We went to church and heard about him. All true. Yet there is a more intimate knowledge of God that comes from experience. We work and play and talk with God. We get to know him better. But ultimately, knowledge of God comes as a gift. He lets us know him. He reveals himself to us in Scripture, in the life of the church, and in the dailiness of living. Most of all, we see him in the smiling face of Jesus.

"Open our eyes to see you, Lord Jesus."

MARCH 9

HYMN

Come, Lord, Thy power alone
The work of grace can do;
Now let it consecrate to Thee
Our hearts and lives anew.

SCRIPTURE

Even before he made the world, God loved us and chose us in Christ to be holy and without fault in his eyes (Ephesians 1:4).

MEDITATION

What does it mean to be chosen, predestined, and called? Many Christians think calling means that God has specific choices in mind for our family life, occupation, and home. Some think he guides them directly in every choice of the day. I have no doubt that God guides, but he has chosen us not so he can make every decision in our lives, but so he can shape us into the kind of people he wants. "He chose us to be holy and blameless in his sight."

"Holy." It's a church word we don't use much elsewhere. "Holy" may conjure up ideas of hypocrisy and outward piety in our minds. Instead, Scripture makes clear that holiness is another word for the character of God. "You be holy for I am Holy," is God's constant refrain in the book of Leviticus. God wants us to share his character. To be as loving and just and merciful and good as he is. This is the choice he makes for us.

"Lord, through your power consecrate us and make us holy as you are holy."

MARCH 10

HYMN

Be ours, with fervent zeal, Till at Thy feet we lay it down,

Thy bloodstained cross to bear; A crown of life to wear.

SCRIPTURE

God blesses those who patiently endure testing and temptation. Afterward they will receive the crown of life that God has promised to those who love him (James 1:12).

MEDITATION

Endurance.

I recently watched a movie about hiking the Appalachian Trail. Each year thousands of hikers take five to seven months to walk over 2100 miles of the trail. I admire this from afar for I can't imagine the mental strength it takes to complete the hike.

Walking with Jesus is also about endurance. No matter how tough it gets, we continue. We place one foot in front of the other. We abide. We endure. We take up the cross daily.

At the end of the journey is the crown of life, not the crown kings wear, but the crown or garland of leaves for victors in ancient athletic contests. We are not in competition with others in our long journey of faith. We win by finishing. We abide. We endure.

"Jesus who endured the cross, give us strength to endure so we also might win."

MARCH
11

HYMN

Refresh our waiting souls,

Our feeble faith inspire,

And from Thine altar touch our hearts

With coals of sacred fire.

SCRIPTURE

Then one of the seraphim flew to me with a burning coal he had taken from the altar with a pair of tongs. He touched my lips with it and said, "See, this coal has touched your lips. Now your guilt is removed, and your sins are forgiven" (Isaiah 6:6-7).

MEDITATION

What saps our strength on our journey with the Lord? Our guilt and shame. Like Isaiah, we are part of a sinful people who do not deserve to see the Lord of Heaven's Armies.

But God takes away our guilt and shame. He burns them away with his fire. Through the life, death, and resurrection of Jesus we are made right with God. His Holy Spirit burns within our hearts, confirming that we are God's beloved children.

This is such good news that it's hard to believe. And so we ask the Lord to inspire our feeble faith and to renew our waiting souls. We ask for strength for one more day to walk with him. We rely on his power, not our own. We ask for the fire of his love.

"Lord, burn us with your fire. Give us trust and power."

MARCH 12

HYMN

All the way my Savior leads me; What have I to ask beside? Can I doubt His tender mercy, Who through life has been my guide?

SCRIPTURE

Surround me with your tender mercies so I may live, for your instructions are my delight (Psalm 119:77).

MEDITATION

I ask a great deal of Jesus. I want him to make me happy, keep me healthy, and bless my family and friends. I want him to give me useful work to do and at the same time make everything fun. I want him to make people like me.

If all this sounds shallow, it is. But I don't think I'm alone. We all expect much from Jesus.

Or not. Perhaps we do not expect too much from Jesus, but too little. We want him to fix everything in our lives, but what he gives is even more. He agrees to lead us all the way. Dare we ask more than this, that he will continue to guide us by his tender mercies? Is that not all that he asks of us as his disciples? "Come follow me." With that we should be content.

"Teacher and Guide, make us content to follow. Give us trust in your tender mercies."

MARCH 13

HYMN

Heav'nly peace, divinest comfort,
Here by faith in Him to dwell!
For I know, whate'er befall me,
Jesus doeth all things well.

SCRIPTURE

They were completely amazed and said again and again, "Everything he does is wonderful. He even makes the deaf to hear and gives speech to those who cannot speak" (Mark 7:37).

MEDITATION

Dare we trust our whole lives with Jesus? Don't we usually rely on him only when we need him, only when we are desperate and cannot handle things ourselves? After all, most of the time we can do fine without him. We are healthy, have good jobs, and are relatively happy. Our families are well, we have enough to eat, and life is good.

Then disaster strikes. Then we turn to Jesus.

Why don't we trust him to guide us even when things are good? Perhaps because we are not convinced that he does all things well. He is even better than we are at the things we think we do well. So whatever happens, good and bad, we give up control to the one who does all things wonderfully.

"Master, may we surrender our whole selves to you."

MARCH
14

HYMN

All the way my Savior leads me, Gives me grace for every trial,

Cheers each winding path I tread; Feeds me with the living bread.

SCRIPTURE

"I am the living bread that came down from heaven. Anyone who eats this bread will live forever; and this bread, which I will offer so the world may live, is my flesh" (John 6:51).

MEDITATION

Bread. In recent years in some circles, bread has gotten a bad reputation.

Even if you avoid bread to be healthy, for most places, in most times bread was what kept you alive. That's why we pray, "Give us this day our daily bread." And we know that prayer is for more than just bread. God provides all our food. He provides all we need. He sustains our life.

But wait, there's more! Jesus promises a deeper, fuller, richer life, a life greater than the best meal we've ever eaten. He gives himself as living bread-- the most mouth-watering, most filling, most nutritious meal ever. His flesh feeds the world.

"Jesus, make us hungry for you. Father, give us this bread daily."

MARCH 15

HYMN

Though my weary steps may falter,

And my soul athirst may be,

Gushing from the rock before me,

Lo! A spring of joy I see;

SCRIPTURE

"But those who drink the water I give will never be thirsty again. It becomes a fresh, bubbling spring within them, giving them eternal life" (John 4:14).

MEDITATION

Of course, I have been thirsty. But I've never been really thirsty. I have seen such thirst in movies—in the desert, lips cracked and bleeding, no water in sight. You can live many days without food, but only a few without water.

I've never had that thirst, but I have had a thirsty soul, a dryness of the spirit that frantically searches for joy and meaning.

Jesus promises to quench that thirst. As living water, he satisfies our profound yearnings for meaning, for purpose, for relationship, for love. Nothing in this world can completely fill our bone-dry souls. In the desert of life, we long for that life-giving refreshment. Jesus really satisfies.

"Water of Life, may we drain the glass of your love this day."

MARCH 16

HYMN

All the way my Savior leads me
O the fullness of His love!
Perfect rest to me is promised
In my Father's house above.

SCRIPTURE

So there is a special rest still waiting for the people of God (Hebrews 4:9).

MEDITATION

Our age thrives on busyness. We have too much to do and not enough time to do it. We overschedule ourselves and even our children. We are tired, worn out, and burned out.

We can even be overly burdened with our life with God. One more church service, ministry opportunity, or daily devotional reading strains us to the breaking point. Rest? It's not an option. How can it be when we have so much to do? We'll rest when we die.

Jesus gives rest. Not just after we die, but now. When God's people turned rest into a burden, not a joy, Jesus said, "The Sabbath was made to meet the needs of people, and not people to meet the requirements of the Sabbath" (Mark 2:27). Jesus gives rest now if only we would receive that gift. He also promises rest, a life with him, in his Father's house. He leads us not into toilsome work, but into peaceful rest.

"Lord, slow us down. May we gratefully receive your gift of rest."

MARCH
17

HYMN

When my spirit, clothed immortal,

Wings its flight to realms of day

This my song through endless ages

Jesus led me all the way;

SCRIPTURE

For our dying bodies must be transformed into bodies that will never die; our mortal bodies must be transformed into immortal bodies (1 Corinthians 15:53).

MEDITATION

Far be it from me to disagree with Fanny Crosby. I also want to give her room for a poetic license. But the Bible makes it clear that Jesus leads us ultimately not to life as immortal spirits but to a new heaven and earth with resurrected bodies.

God could have led us only through his Spirit. But "the Word became human and made his home among us." God took on a body. That body died and was raised from the dead. Jesus bodily ascended into heaven and will return in his resurrected body. What's more, we will be given immortal resurrection bodies. And in those bodies, we will sing, "Jesus led me all the way."

What a delight to follow the flesh-and-blood Jesus! To follow him through the cross to glory with the Father!

"Brother Jesus, may we follow and glorify you this day in our bodies."

MARCH
18

HYMN

We cannot fold our hands at ease, / And look for Heav'n at last; / We cannot shout the victory won / Until the war is past.

SCRIPTURE

For we are not fighting against flesh-and-blood enemies, but against evil rulers and authorities of the unseen world, against mighty powers in this dark world, and against evil spirits in the heavenly places (Ephesians 6:12).

MEDITATION

The Bible gives several word pictures of our life with Jesus, including this metaphor of a soldier in the army of God. We are not called to violence but to the virtues of a warrior—loyalty, duty, honor, and courage. Perhaps above all, as Christian soldiers, Jesus calls us to endurance.

Think of all that soldiers must sacrifice. They are separated from the families they love. So Christians also must be ready to leave father, mother, wife, husband, and children (Matthew 19:29). Soldiers often live in harsh conditions with little food and shelter. So do we who follow the one who had nowhere to lay his head (Matthew 8:20). Soldiers endure fatigue, danger, and death. Jesus also demands that we endure. If soldiers endure, they can shout when victory comes.

"Lord of heaven's armies, give us courage to endure."

MARCH 19

HYMN

We cannot hope to win the prize,
Unless the race we run;
Nor reap the fruits of endless joy
If we no work have done.

SCRIPTURE

Don't you realize that in a race everyone runs, but only one person gets the prize? So run to win! All athletes are disciplined in their training. They do it to win a prize that will fade away, but we do it for an eternal prize (1 Corinthians 9:24-25).

MEDITATION

Athletes practice. They run laps. They endure the heat and the cold. They do this for hours each day. Why?

It helps them get stronger and faster. It gives them endurance for the last part of the race or game or match. It gives them confidence. Training allows them to accomplish what they cannot do by simply trying harder. When one is too exhausted to think or to try, muscle memory takes over.

We work hard for Jesus, not to earn salvation, but to train in holiness. We work so our trust in Jesus can endure.

"Jesus, strengthen our weak faith. Give us endurance."

MARCH 20

HYMN

We cannot slumber at our post,
Nor lay our armor down,
And only they who bear the cross
Can ever wear the crown.

SCRIPTURE

When the watchman sees the enemy coming, he sounds the alarm to warn the people (Ezekiel 33:3).

MEDITATION

Christ enlists us to be sentinels or lookouts. Those on watch protect the camp from infiltration by the enemy. Good sentinels stays alert. They fight the urge to doze in the long watches of the night. They take seriously their responsibility to safeguard the vulnerable.

Those who follow Jesus cannot relax their vigilance. Yes, Jesus gives us rest, but it is an attentive rest. We pay attention, listening for the voice of our Commander. We also stay alert for dangers to the flock of the Lord.

This is not an invitation to paranoia and judgmentalism. But we must have our eyes and ears open to the dangers the world places before us. This takes effort, even heroic endurance. We bear the cross of shielding those whose faith is at risk, even at risk to ourselves.

"Great Shepherd, keep us awake to guard your flock."

MARCH 21

HYMN

Then let the cross be all our boast,

And Jesus all our song,

Till in His robe of righteousness

We join the ransomed throng.

SCRIPTURE

As for me, may I never boast about anything except the cross of our Lord Jesus Christ. Because of that cross, my interest in this world has been crucified, and the world's interest in me has also died (Galatians 6:14).

MEDITATION

We've all been taught it's wrong to boast or brag. Yet we do. Why?

Because everybody wants to be somebody.

What makes us somebody? Usually, we think we must accomplish something to be somebody. We must be better at something in order to truly count.

It is the cross of Christ that makes us somebody. By sheer grace, Jesus gave himself for us so that we might be God's beloved children. It is what he accomplished, not what we accomplished.

So we can brag and boast. We are somebody. We are his body.

"Lord Jesus, move us from competition to gratitude."

MARCH
22

HYMN

Blessed are they that endure to the end, For with them it shall be well; They shall eat of the fruit of the tree of life, And with Jesus forever dwell.

SCRIPTURE

To everyone who is victorious I will give fruit from the tree of life in the paradise of God (Revelation 2:7).

MEDITATION

The tree of life is in Eden, giving life to humanity (Genesis 2:9). When humans rebel against God, doing things their way, God blocks their way to the tree of life (Genesis 3:24). But the tree of life returns in the new heaven and earth, when the leaves of the tree are "used for medicine to heal the nations" (see Revelation 22:1-3).

How marvelous to have a tree that heals all our diseases. To have fruit that gives new life. To see the nations healed from their conflicts.

Christians through the ages have connected this tree to another tree, the cross of Christ. The cross was a tree that brought a cursed death, "Cursed is everyone who is hung on a tree" (Galatians 3:13, Deuteronomy 21:23). But the power of God brought life out of death.

"Jesus, help us to endure through the life-giving power of the cross."

MARCH 23

HYMN

Jesus, keep me near the cross,

There a precious fountain

Free to all, a healing stream

Flows from Calvary's mountain.

SCRIPTURE

One of the soldiers, however, pierced his side with a spear, and immediately blood and water flowed out (John 19:34).

MEDITATION

I'm not very fond of seeing blood, particularly my own. Although the Bible clearly says we are cleansed by the blood of Jesus, I've always had mixed feelings about that picture.

That's why it helps me to see the blood of Jesus as a "healing stream." I can relate to being healed by blood. The Red Cross reminds us that giving blood not only helps those who have surgery but also those with injuries or ongoing illnesses like cancer.

The blood of Jesus heals, not as a literal transfusion, but as the power that restores our relationship with God. It also heals our broken bonds with other people and with creation. That life-giving stream flows from the cross to us and through us to others.

So, let us rejoice with gratitude for our health!

"Lamb of God, heal us by your blood."

MARCH 24

HYMN

Near the cross, a trembling soul,
Love and mercy found me;
There the bright and morning star
Sheds its beams around me.

SCRIPTURE

Because of that experience, we have even greater confidence in the message proclaimed by the prophets. You must pay close attention to what they wrote, for their words are like a lamp shining in a dark place—until the Day dawns, and Christ the Morning Star shines in your hearts (2 Peter 1:19).

MEDITATION

When Jesus was on the cross, "darkness fell across the whole land" (Luke 23:44).

It was the darkest day in history, a day when it looked as though the forces of evil completely triumphed.

But out of that darkness came the brightest light. God brought victory from defeat, raising Jesus from the dead. Even on the cross, Jesus was the morning star, the last star we see before the dawn breaks and daylight comes. That star is near us, even when we carry our crosses.

"Morning Star, shine on us today. Turn defeat into victory."

MARCH
25

HYMN

Near the cross! O Lamb of God, / Help me walk from day to day,

Bring its scenes before me; / With its shadows o'er me.

SCRIPTURE

Then he said to the crowd, "If any of you wants to be my follower, you must give up your own way, take up your cross daily, and follow me" (Luke 9:23).

MEDITATION

When God sent his beloved Son in to the world, he sent him not with the trappings of power and greatness. Jesus is born in a stable, not a palace. He lives not in Jerusalem, the city of God, but in Nazareth, in Galilee (can anything good come from there?). He is raised not by priests or Bible scholars but by a carpenter. He begins his ministry not with a spectacular miracle, but with an act of repentance. Though without sin, he joins the sinners in baptism.

At every fork in the road, Jesus chooses failure over success, service over leadership, goodness over greatness. He even chooses the cross. Yes, he prays, "Let his cup pass," but he also adds, "Not my will but yours be done." He lets the Father lead him to the cross.

Will we do the same?

"Jesus, keep us near the cross each day."

MARCH 26

HYMN

Near the cross I'll watch and wait   Till I reach the golden strand,

Hoping, trusting ever,   Just beyond the river.

SCRIPTURE

Standing near the cross were Jesus' mother, and his mother's sister, Mary (the wife of Clopas), and Mary Magdalene (John 19:25).

MEDITATION

Try to imagine what it would be like to see your son suffer on a cross. What must have gone through the mind of these women as they witnessed his agony?

Surely, they prayed, "Let this stop, now." They must have thought that this was the end of Jesus and his claims to be Messiah. The death of hope.

But three days later, some of these women were at an empty tomb. Then they saw the risen Jesus. Mary, the mother of Jesus, went from seeing him on the cross to seeing him come in glory in the Holy Spirit (Acts 1:14).

At the cross, these women had to be hoping and trusting ever. They had to live by faith, not sight. So do we.

"Jesus, give us the trust to watch and wait in hope."

MARCH 27

HYMN

In the cross, in the cross,

Be my glory ever;

Till my raptured soul shall find

Rest beyond the river.

SCRIPTURE

The message of the cross is foolish to those who are headed for destruction! But we who are being saved know it is the very power of God (1 Corinthians 1:18).

MEDITATION

Crosses. You see them everywhere. On churches. On hospitals. People wear them around their necks—gold crosses, silver crosses, diamond crosses.

In our day the cross is a fashion accessory or a symbol of Christianity.

In Jesus's day, the cross meant a shameful death, reserved only for the worst of criminals. No wonder many in that day thought it foolish to follow a crucified leader. How can a dead Messiah help us?

Even today, many cannot fathom how self-sacrificing love is more powerful than violent aggression. How can we fight injustice without a bigger, faster gun?

But we know the power of the cross. In its shame is our glory.

"Jesus, may we rest in the cross, trusting its power of love."

MARCH
28

HYMN

Christ hath risen! Hallelujah!
Blessed morn of life and light!
Lo, the grave is rent asunder,
Death is conquered through His might.

SCRIPTURE

But thank God! He gives us victory over sin and death through our Lord Jesus Christ (1 Corinthians 15:57).

MEDITATION

On the cross, death kills death.

That makes no sense without resurrection. When Jesus is raised from the dead, it is more than just one man coming back to life. This is not resuscitation but resurrection. A new kind of life, not completely different from the old, but different in significant ways.

Jesus is raised never to die again. And he is the first of many to experience this new life. We have been raised with Christ in baptism. Through the Spirit, he gives us new life every day. And our bodies will be raised to be like his—incorruptible, never to age and break down, never to die.

Death is real but it is not final. Death itself will die.

"Resurrected Savior, may we trust your defeat of death."

MARCH
29

HYMN

Christ hath risen! Hallelujah!   He is now the King of glory,

He hath risen, as He said;   And our great exalted Head.

SCRIPTURE

Christ is also the head of the church, which is his body. He is the beginning, supreme over all who rise from the dead. So he is first in everything (Colossians 1:18).

MEDITATION

"First in everything."

It sounds like what an overly proud father or mother would say about their child.

But with Jesus, it is no exaggeration. Of course, as the Son of God, Jesus was always first in everything. But he gave that up. He humbled himself to be human like us. And to be human means one is not first in everything. Perhaps first in some things, but not in everything.

So how did Christ become the head, first in everything? By becoming like us. By giving up everything. By dying the shameful death of the cross. But (most of all) by being raised from the dead. He leads the march to resurrection for all.

"Head of all things, first in everything, raise us up with you."

MARCH
30

HYMN

Christ is risen! Hallelujah!

Gladness fills the world today;

From the tomb that could not hold Him, See, the stone is rolled away!

SCRIPTURE

But the angel said, "Don't be alarmed. You are looking for Jesus of Nazareth, who was crucified. He isn't here! He is risen from the dead! Look, this is where they laid his body" (Mark 16:6).

MEDITATION

Imagine that you bring flowers to the grave of someone you love, only to find the grave empty. What would you feel?

Anger? Someone has desecrated the grave. Puzzled? What happened to the body? Where did they take it? Afraid? Graves are eerie places at the best of times, but empty graves that should hold a body are particularly scary.

The women at the tomb of Jesus must have felt all this and more. What they did not feel was joy at the empty tomb, at least not at first. Despite all that Jesus had said, they did not expect his tomb to be empty.

Joy only comes when they believe in angelic messengers who proclaim the resurrection.

"Lord of the empty tomb, give us faith in the message of resurrection."

MARCH
31

HYMN

Christ, the Lord, is risen today,   Hallelujah, hallelujah,

He is risen indeed.   Hallelujah, Amen.

SCRIPTURE

He isn't here! He is risen from the dead! (Luke 24:6).

MEDITATION

I've been blessed to travel through much of the world and hear God's people praise him in many languages. Often, I could not understand a word of that praise, except for one word.

"Hallelujah."

It's a Hebrew word known by all who know our God. It means, "Praise the Lord." Of course, many use the word as an interjection of joy, not knowing its meaning. But for followers of Jesus, that single word weighs significance. We praise the Lord God because he created the world, he made a covenant with his people, he kept the covenant when his people broke it, he became flesh and lived among us, and he died for our sins.

Yet our loudest "Hallelujah" comes when we confess that Jesus is risen, he is risen indeed.

"Praise the Lord for resurrection!"

APRIL 1

HYMN

"He captive led captivity,   He broke the bars of death,

He robbed the grave of victory,"   He broke the bars of death.

SCRIPTURE

"The Spirit of the Lord is upon me, for he has anointed me to bring Good News to the poor. He has sent me to proclaim that captives will be released, that the blind will see, that the oppressed will be set free, and that the time of the Lord's favor has come" (Luke 4:18-19).

MEDITATION

"Jail break!"

Not too long ago, armed police showed up in our neighborhood telling us to stay in our homes because an escaped criminal was in the area. We did not relax until he had been captured. Dangerous criminals should be locked up safely behind bars.

Release of captives doesn't sound like a good thing.

Unless you are a captive.

And that's what we were. Captive to sin and death, we had no hope of release. Until the resurrection. The bars of death that held us were broken. Jesus brought us sweet freedom.

"Victorious Jesus, may we live the good news of our release."

APRIL 2

HYMN

Let every mourning soul rejoice,
And sing with one united voice;
The Savior rose today,
The Savior rose today.

SCRIPTURE

Jesus told her, "I am the resurrection and the life. Anyone who believes in me will live, even after dying" (John 11:25).

MEDITATION

"Jesus wept" (John 11:35).

As kids, when we were told to choose a Bible verse to memorize, this is the one we would pick, the shortest verse in the Bible. Later, looking at the verse in context, it at first made no sense. Jesus knows he is about to raise Lazarus from the dead. Still, he cries over him.

Why? There is something contagious about grief. When those we love are hurting, we hurt too. So Jesus weeps with those who weep.

When Jesus tells Martha her brother Lazarus will rise again, she believes he will rise on the last day. Jesus makes it clear that the last day has already arrived. "I am the resurrection and the life." Jesus turns weeping into joy. Resurrection comes today.

"Master, may we believe in you as the resurrection and life."

APRIL 3

HYMN

The great and glorious work is done,

Free grace to all thro' Christ, the Son;

Hosanna to His name,

Hosanna to His name.

SCRIPTURE

God saved you by his grace when you believed. And you can't take credit for this; it is a gift from God (Ephesians 2:8).

MEDITATION

The phrase "Free grace" is redundant. Grace by definition is always free. Many Christians but stipulations on grace. One of the prayers I frequently heard in my youth said, "When we've done all that we can do, give us a home in heaven with you."

But have we ever done all that we can do? And even if we have, will that move God to give us a home with him? No. It's all by grace.

The resurrection makes it clear that grace is free. Jesus could not raise himself; he had to trust the Father to raise him. We cannot raise ourselves; we have to trust the power and grace of God.

Free grace to all. This is the message of resurrection.

"Jesus, thank you for your finished work of free grace to all."

APRIL 4

HYMN

Simply trusting all the way,

Taking Jesus at His word;

Simply trusting, when I pray,

Every promise of my Lord.

SCRIPTURE

Faith shows the reality of what we hope for; it is the evidence of things we cannot see (Hebrews 11:1).

MEDITATION

"Trust me."

Whenever I hear those words, I immediately place my hand on my wallet to make sure it is still there. I find it hard to trust because many use trust to manipulate, to rob, and to scam.

Jesus says, "Trust me."

Our relation to God through Christ is not a matter of certainty based on what we see with our own eyes and know with our reason. It is a certainty based on trust. Yes, we have reasons to trust Jesus. We have the witness of Scripture. We have the testimony of those who have trusted Jesus before us. We have our experience of the blessings Jesus gives.

But it still is a matter of simply trusting.

"Jesus, increase our trust in your words and promises."

APRIL

5

HYMN

Trusting when my sky is bright,
Trusting when my heart is glad;

Trusting in the gloom of night,
When my every thought is sad.

SCRIPTURE

The Lord is close to the brokenhearted; he rescues those whose spirits are crushed (Psalm 34:18).

MEDITATION

We trust in Jesus. But we also have doubts. Often it is the disappointments in life that make us doubt. If Jesus is truly with us, why do we have this pain, this disease, this betrayal, this loss?

There are no easy answers to that question. God does not often show us the reasons for suffering. But God does promise, through Christ and the Holy Spirit, to be with us in our disappointment. We follow one who knew suffering and grief.

So we look for God in all the events of life—good and bad. It's easy to see his hand in the blessings. It is much harder when we feel we are cursed, not blessed. In those times when we cannot see, we trust. It does not look like it, but God is still there.

This is not shallow optimism, looking on the bright side and slapping on a happy face. It is a profoundly deep conviction that God loves us.

"God of love, increase our trust when times are bad."

APRIL 6

HYMN

Trusting when 'tis well with me,   Trusting Jesus' love for me,

Trusting whatsoe'er befall;   Simply trusting, that is all.

SCRIPTURE

This is real love—not that we loved God, but that he loved us and sent his Son as a sacrifice to take away our sins (1 John 4:10).

MEDITATION

Many of us have trouble believing that we are loved. Perhaps that's because we have been deeply wounded by those who should have loved us but did not. Perhaps it's because we know our own faults so deeply that we are overcome with guilt and shame. Who could love us?

Jesus loves me. It's not just a children's song, it's the most profound truth. He loves us not because we are so lovable, but because God is love.

But how can we trust the love of God when it seems he has abandoned us? We rely on memory. We repeat the story— "For God so loved the world...." We remember who we are, God's beloved. We confess, especially when we do not feel it, "I am loved by God."

It is a love on which we can depend.

"This day when I feel unloved and unlovable, give me trust in your love, Jesus."

APRIL 7

HYMN

Simply trusting, simply trusting, To the cross of Christ I cling;
Trusting Jesus, that is all; Simply trusting, that is all.

SCRIPTURE

I cling to you; your strong right hand holds me securely (Psalm 63:8).

MEDITATION

I never liked folks who were clingy, who would not give me my space. "Cling" is not a good word for me.

Instead, I substitute "hold on." Like someone falling off a cliff is told by their rescuer, "Hold on!" Like a drowning person is thrown the lifebuoy and told "Hold on."

Sometimes all we can do is hold on. We are at the end of our rope. There seems no way out of our desperation. The situation overwhelms us. Then the voice comes. Hold on, Don't give up. Endure.

And what we are thrown to hold on to is not a rope or a lifejacket. It's a cross. We "keep our eyes on Jesus, who endured the cross, disregarding its shame" (Hebrew 12:2). He will rescue us by that cross. Hold on.

"Jesus, come to our aid. Hurry to help us."

APRIL 8

HYMN

Praise Him, praise Him   Sing, O earth,

Jesus, our blessed Redeemer,   His wonderful love proclaim.

SCRIPTURE

All glory to him who alone is God, our Savior through Jesus Christ our Lord. All glory, majesty, power, and authority are his before all time, and in the present, and beyond all time! Amen (Jude 25).

MEDITATION

Why does God deserve praise? Because God is our Creator, our Father, our Provider.

Why does Jesus deserve praise? Because he is God—Creator, Father, and Provider. He has all glory, majesty, power, and authority. What's more, God's wonderful love became flesh in Jesus. In his every word and action, we see the love of God embodied.

Jesus is our Savior, our redeemer. When we were in dire straits with no hope, he rescued us. No amount of effort on our part or self-improvement could save us. Only Jesus, our blessed Redeemer.

And that redemption is not only for us but for the whole earth.

"Jesus, we join with the whole earth to praise you as Redeemer."

APRIL 9

HYMN

Hail Him! hail Him! highest archangels in glory; Strength and honor give to His holy name!

SCRIPTURE

And when he brought his supreme Son into the world, God said, "Let all of God's angels worship him" (Hebrews 1:6).

MEDITATION

When angels appear in the Bible they always say the same thing. "Do not be afraid!"

Why? Why are angels so scary? Well, they are supernatural beings. That's scary in itself. What's more, they come from the Presence of the Almighty God. They reflect God's frightening majesty.

Yet these angels praise and worship Jesus. They appear to announce both his birth and his resurrection. Even archangels (who must be the scariest of all) fall down at the feet of the resurrected Jesus in glory.

If angels are frightening, then Jesus is more so. Not frightening in a threatening way but frightening because of the depth of his redeeming love.

"Jesus, we tremble at the power of your holy name."

APRIL
10

HYMN

Like a shepherd,   In His arms

Jesus will guard His children,   He carries them all day long.

SCRIPTURE

"I am the good shepherd. The good shepherd sacrifices his life for the sheep" (John 10:11).

MEDITATION

Shepherding seems like such a gentle occupation, spending time with those sweet and fluffy sheep.

It is actually quite dangerous. Shepherds work in threatening weather. They work long hours, with really no time off. And they face dangerous predators. David as shepherd had to fight off lions and bears with just a club (see 1 Samuel 17:33–37).

Jesus faces the dangers of being our shepherd. He provides shelter and food. He protects us from enemies. He even gives his life for us, his sheep.

And he does this willingly and gladly. "Because of the joy awaiting him, he endured the cross, disregarding its shame" (Hebrews 12:2). He gave his arms to be nailed to the cross so he could cradle us in those same arms.

"Give us grace to rest in your arms, Shepherd Jesus."

APRIL 11

HYMN

O ye saints that dwell on the mountain of Zion, Praise Him, praise Him ever in joyful song.

SCRIPTURE

No, you have come to Mount Zion, to the city of the living God, the heavenly Jerusalem, and to countless thousands of angels in a joyful gathering (Hebrews 12:22).

MEDITATION

Zion is mentioned over 150 times in the Bible and also found in many hymns. A hill outside of Jerusalem, David captured Mount Zion and soon the city around it became the City of David (2 Samuel 5:7). Later, Zion means all Jerusalem, especially the Temple, as "the city of the Great King."

Israel made pilgrimages to Zion to be in the presence of the Lord. Zion later takes on a spiritual significance, separate from its physical location. Zion is the place where God lives. We who follow Jesus have come to Zion, the heavenly Jerusalem, the very presence of God.

When we praise, when we pray, at every moment of the day we enter Zion. Through Christ we have a personal, intimate, cherished bond with the Almighty.

"We praise you Jesus, for opening the way to Zion."

APRIL 12

HYMN

Praise Him, praise Him
Jesus, our blessed Redeemer,
For our sins
He suffered, and bled, and died.

SCRIPTURE

Christ suffered for our sins once for all time. He never sinned, but he died for sinners to bring you safely home to God. He suffered physical death, but he was raised to life in the Spirit (1 Peter 3:18).

MEDITATION

The other day I passed a sign that said, "Redemption Center." I thought, "That's a creative name for a church."

It was not a church but a business that bought back recyclable bottles and cans.

Which reminded me of the real meaning of redemption. Our relationship with Jesus is personal. It is more than a transaction.

Yet redemption is a transactional word. Jesus buys us back from slavery to sin. He redeems us with the great price of his death on the cross. Since he bought us, we belong to him. Every part of us, every thought, every action is to his glory.

"Buyer Jesus, we praise you as Redeemer. May we give full value today."

APRIL 13

HYMN

He our rock,

our hope of eternal salvation,

Hail Him, hail Him,

Jesus the Crucified.

SCRIPTURE

And all of them drank the same spiritual water. For they drank from the spiritual rock that traveled with them, and that rock was Christ (1 Corinthians 10:4).

MEDITATION

What words come to mind when you think of a "rock"? Hard. Stable. Lasting.

God is often called our rock in the Bible. He is ever-lasting. We can depend on him. Rock also referred to a refuge or fortress. God is our mighty fortress. Then there are the biblical stories of God bringing water from the rock for Israel in the desert (Exodus 17:1–7; Numbers 20:1–14).

A rock that is faithful, that protects, that provides. This is our God.

Jesus is our faithful rock that protects and provides. Our hope in him is rock-solid.

But Jesus is also described as a rock that makes some stumble (Romans 9:33 quoting Isaiah 28:16). Will we trip up on Jesus or will we trust him?

"Jesus, our Rock, may we depend on your faithful provision today."

HYMN

Loving Savior, meekly enduring sorrow,

Crowned with thorns that cruelly pierced His brow;

Once for us rejected, despised and forsaken,

Prince of Glory, He is triumphant now.

SCRIPTURE

You are coming to Christ, who is the living cornerstone of God's temple. He was rejected by people, but he was chosen by God for great honor (1 Peter 2:4).

MEDITATION

We all know what it's like to be rejected. It happened when we were turned down for a date or when somebody broke up with us. It might be our own family—father, mother, children—who rejected us. To offer another love and then have it thrown in our face can hurt for a lifetime.

Even though we all know what it's like to be rejected, it's hard to imagine anyone rejecting the love of a God who gave his Son. It's unthinkable that some would reject Jesus, the loving Savior. But they did. And they do.

Do we?

"Loving Jesus, may we accept your gift of love this day and share that gift with others."

APRIL
15

HYMN

Praise Him, praise Him Heav'nly portals
Jesus, our blessed Redeemer, loud with hosannas ring.

SCRIPTURE

And then I heard every creature in heaven and on earth and under the earth and in the sea. They sang: "Blessing and honor and glory and power belong to the one sitting on the throne and to the Lamb forever and ever" (Revelation 5:13).

MEDITATION

Many religious worship the earth as a goddess under different names—Gaia, Mother Earth, and others. This is somewhat understandable since we depend on the earth for our life.

And yet we don't. We depend on the God who made and the Savior who redeemed the earth. We worship the Creator, not the creatures. Indeed, all the created order worships the One who sits upon the throne and the Lamb.

We might not think we are liable to worship the earth, but we are bombarded with ads that claim that some created thing will bring us fulfillment. We must fight greed and materialism so we may join in the songs of praise from all creation.

"Almighty God, Redeeming Lamb, may we join the song of praise."

APRIL
16

HYMN

Jesus, Savior, reigneth forever and ever.

Crown Him! Crown Him Prophet, and Priest, and King!

SCRIPTURE

On his robe at his thigh was written this title: King of all kings and Lord of all lords (Revelation 19:16).

MEDITATION

Jesus is King. Those of us who live in democracies do not want a king, at least not one with power. Power is in the people. We do not want anyone to tell us how to live. But Jesus has all authority and demands complete obedience.

Jesus is Prophet. He speaks for God. But we tend to distrust anyone who claims to speak from God. We want to question and doubt their words. Jesus will not be doubted.

Jesus is Priest. He sacrifices for sin. But we misunderstand the priesthood of all believers to mean we can act as our own priest. Jesus is the one who brings us to God. We don't do it ourselves.

Crowning Jesus Prophet, Priest, and King means removing ourselves from the throne.

"King Jesus, we bow, we trust, we rely on you alone."

APRIL 17

HYMN

Death is vanquished!
Tell it with joy, ye faithful.

Where is now thy victory, boasting grave?

SCRIPTURE

Then, when our dying bodies have been transformed into bodies that will never die, this Scripture will be fulfilled: "Death is swallowed up in victory. O death, where is your victory? O death, where is your sting?" (1 Corinthians 15:54-55).

MEDITATION

Death is not the way things are supposed to be. We forget that sometimes. When we stand at the grave of someone we love, death seems so final. We even get used to it, saying, "Death is just a part of life."

But when God made humans and put them in the garden, he gave them access to the tree of life. Only after they rebelled against God's way were they denied access to that tree (see Genesis 3:22-24). Through another tree, the cross, Jesus the Son of God opened the way again to the tree of life. The healing tree of life will return. (Revelation 22:2-14).

So death is real, but it is not final.

"God of life, increase our trust in the reality of the resurrection."

APRIL 18

HYMN

Jesus lives! No longer thy portals are cheerless;

Jesus lives, the mighty and strong to save.

SCRIPTURE

And God will raise us from the dead by his power, just as he raised our Lord from the dead (1 Corinthians 6:14).

MEDITATION

I believe in the resurrection of Jesus. I have more trouble believing in my own resurrection. That is not just a lack of faith on my part, but also a lack of imagination. Why doesn't God just tell us what it will be like?

Imagine that an unborn child has an adult understanding. How would you describe the world to her? How could you get her to understand colors, cold, beauty, and tastes? How could you allow him to grasp interaction with other people?

You could not. The child literally could not imagine.

So with us, this world, like the womb, seems so familiar and comfortable that it's hard to imagine a better world that is both different and the same. But we trust the power of Jesus.

"Resurrected Jesus, open our eyes of the beauty of life with you."

APRIL 19

HYMN

Source from whence the stream of mercy

Like a river flows to me,

With Thy cords of love so tender

Bind and keep me close to Thee.

SCRIPTURE

I led Israel along with my ropes of kindness and love. I lifted the yoke from his neck, and I myself stooped to feed him (Hosea 11:4).

MEDITATION

Being bound with cords or ropes does not sound enjoyable to me, although it might to some.

In the Bible, being tied up means one is helpless and in danger. Abraham binds Isaac to be a sacrifice (Genesis 22:9). Delilah binds Samson (Judges 16). Nebuchadnezzar orders Shadrach, Meshach and Abed-nego to be bound and thrown into the furnace of blazing fire (Daniel 3:20).

God binds us to him and him to us with cords of love. It's an interesting picture. We are tied to the Almighty. We cannot escape him. What's more, he ties himself to us, not to make us helpless, but to give us help.

"Bind us close to you this day, God of kindness and love."

APRIL
20

HYMN

There my life, my hope and comfort,

There a refuge for my soul,

When the clouds hang darkly round me,

And the distant surges roll.

SCRIPTURE

The Lord is a shelter for the oppressed, a refuge in times of trouble (Psalm 9:9).

MEDITATION

When I was a kid, the boys in our neighborhood built a hideout. It was the secret place where we could do what we wanted without parental interference.

Hideouts were big in old Westerns. It kept the outlaws safe from the law.

Even as adults, we need a hideout, a safe place. We are not hiding from parents or the law, but we do seek a place where we can be ourselves and where trouble cannot find us. Victims of abuse need a safe place.

Our God is the ultimate safe place, a hideout from all the dark, malevolent forces outside and inside us. The Almighty is stronger than any challenge we face. We can rest safely in his love.

"Solid Refuge, let us hide ourselves in you this day."

APRIL 21

HYMN

There in holy, sweet communion
With Thy Spirit day by day,
Faith to realms of light and glory
Bears my raptured soul away.

SCRIPTURE

The Spirit of God, who raised Jesus from the dead, lives in you. And just as God raised Christ Jesus from the dead, he will give life to your mortal bodies by this same Spirit living within you (Romans 8:11).

MEDITATION

God himself is with us. This is more than a figure of speech. It is more than having God in our thoughts and mind. Almighty God lives within us through the Holy Spirit.

Jesus himself is with us. This is more than simply following the example of Jesus. The Jesus who walked the earth in a body continues to walk the earth in our bodies. All by the Spirit.

There's something spooky about the Spirit. In the King James Version, he's even called the "Holy Ghost." But by "spooky" I don't mean ghostly. I mean that the indwelling of the Spirit is supernatural. It's not about feeling spiritual. It's not always about dramatic events from the Spirit. It's about trusting the Presence of Father, Son, and Spirit.

"This day, may we experience sweet communion with your Holy Spirit."

APRIL 22

HYMN

Close to Thee, O Savior, keep me,

Till I reach the shining shore,

Till I join the raptured army,

Shouting joy forevermore.

SCRIPTURE

For we are not fighting against flesh-and-blood enemies, but against evil rulers and authorities of the unseen world, against mighty powers in this dark world, and against evil spirits in the heavenly places (Ephesians 6:12).

MEDITATION

"Beat'em and Beat'em Bad!"

That's what my friend Chuck Ross, sports fanatic, used to say. You might not like his grammar, but you may share his sentiment when your favorite sports team plays their hated rival.

We also are in a contest, a war not against people but against dark powers of evil.

The good news is "God's team wins." I hope that does not trivialize the battle. Injustice, violence, and oppression seem to rule our world. But they do not. The Lord God reigns. Jesus defeats the vile wickedness of cosmic forces by dying on the cross and being raised from the dead. He beat them badly. By staying close to him, we are on the winning side.

"Triumphant Jesus, keep us close to you in the battle."

APRIL 23

HYMN

Savior, more than life to me,

I am clinging, clinging, close to Thee;

Let Thy precious blood applied,

Keep me ever, ever near Thy side.

SCRIPTURE

I cling to you; your strong right hand holds me securely (Psalm 63:8).

MEDITATION

"Hold me close." They sound like words from a love song. Because they are.

God loves us. Many times, in the Bible that love is compared to the love between a man and a woman. Israel is the Lord's bride. The church is the bride of Christ.

What does it mean to be held close? Certainly, affection and love but also protection. At the edge of a cliff, we want someone to hold us securely.

Jesus holds us in tenderness and protection. He does this by his applied blood, his death for us. What he asks from us is to embrace his embrace, to cling to him. That may sound easy, but in a world that constantly tells us we are not worthy of love, it is not always easy to feel his strong right hand holding us securely.

"Strong and tender Jesus, may we hold tightly to you this day."

APRIL 24

HYMN

Through this changing world below,

Lead me gently, gently as I go;

Trusting Thee, I cannot stray,

I can never, never lose my way.

SCRIPTURE

Jesus Christ is the same yesterday, today, and forever (Hebrews 13:8).

MEDITATION

Like most folks, I like variety. But I also like reliability. It is good to experience new things. It is also good to experience the predictable.

Life in Jesus is new every morning. Our God cannot be controlled. He is in charge, not us. We cannot fully predict his actions.

Yet life in Jesus is predictable. The character of our God is solid, sure, and stable. We know that the Lord will lead us only in green pastures and to still waters. Even though the path seems so precarious and perilous, he leads us only where he has gone before. In a world that is constantly changing, by clinging to him we are sure that we are on the right path. We cannot lose our way when our eyes are fixed on the one who smooths the road before us. Whatever challenges this day may send, he gently guides us.

"In a world of too many choices, may we trust you to lead."

APRIL 25

HYMN

Let me love Thee more and more,

Till this fleeting, fleeting life is o'er;

Till my soul is lost in love,

In a brighter, brighter world above.

SCRIPTURE

How do you know what your life will be like tomorrow? Your life is like the morning fog—it's here a little while, then it's gone (James 4:14).

MEDITATION

"Life is short and then you die."

That was once a popular saying. It was meant to be fatalistic and depressing.

But it is true. Life is short and then you die.

I live near a river and there is heavy fog there most mornings. However, in a short while the sun comes out and the fog disappears. The Bible often compares our brief life to a fog. That puts the day into perspective. This day, this life, is important but it won't last long.

Except in Jesus, it does. He gives not just longer life but eternal life. A new quality of life that will not end. Good news! Life is short and then we have life in a new heaven and earth!

"Jesus, increase our trust in the brighter life you have given and will give."

APRIL 26

HYMN

Every day, every hour,   May Thy tender love to me

Let me feel Thy cleansing power;   Bind me closer, closer, Lord to Thee.

SCRIPTURE

But if we are living in the light, as God is in the light, then we have fellowship with each other, and the blood of Jesus, his Son, cleanses us from all sin (1 John 1:7).

MEDITATION

There are few joys in life greater than a bath or shower. Being clean is a delight we often take for granted.

Oh, to be clean inside! To have sins and worries and doubts washed away. And that's what happened to us at our baptism. We are completely cleansed.

Clean bodies and clothes do not last long. They must be washed again and again. We may feel it's the same with the inner cleansing.

But it is not. We are always baptized people. The cleansing from Jesus is ongoing, it never ends. We cling to that purification every hour and it binds us closer to the God who so loves us.

"Jesus, may we feel your cleansing power every hour of this day."

APRIL
27

HYMN

Will you come, will you come,
With your poor broken heart,
Burdened and sin oppressed?

Lay it down at the feet
Of your Savior and Lord,
Jesus will give you rest.

SCRIPTURE

He heals the brokenhearted and bandages their wounds (Psalm 147:3).

MEDITATION

As I write this, I have a huge multi-colored bruise on my upper arm from a fall I had last week. My arm hurt for a few days but it does not hurt now. The bruise remains.

The wounds of the heart last longer. Sometimes one does not see the damage outwardly, but the pain remains. Sometimes others break our hearts, but the greatest pains are the torments we bring on ourselves through selfish actions. Our hearts hurt because we have wounded others. The heart turns away from God, which brings the greatest hurt of all.

When in pain, we want relief. We crave rest. Who can heal our broken hearts?

We lay our hearts at the feet of the Great Physician. He cures and gives rest.

"Man of Sorrows, mend our broken hearts by your suffering and resurrection."

APRIL 28

HYMN

Will you come, will you come?
There is mercy for you,
Balm for your aching breast;
Only come as you are,
And believe on His name,
Jesus will give you rest.

SCRIPTURE

The Spirit of the Sovereign Lord is upon me, for the Lord has anointed me to bring good news to the poor. He has sent me to comfort the brokenhearted and to proclaim that captives will be released, and prisoners will be freed (Isaiah 61:1).

MEDITATION

"Come as you are." It used to be a common phrase on party invitations, letting those invited know that thy did not have to "dress up" to come.

Jesus invites us to a party, the greatest of all. It's the party that includes the poor, the oppressed and the captive. And he asks us to come as we are! I've known people who say, "I plan to come back to church when I straighten up and get my life together." That's not what Jesus asks of us. He only asks us to come for riches, healing, and peace. He wants us as we are—broken, imprisoned, and hurting.

"Lord of hospitality, may we accept your merciful call."

APRIL 29

HYMN

Will you come, will you come?

You have nothing to pay;

Jesus, who loves you best,

By His death on the cross

Purchased life for your soul,

Jesus will give you rest.

SCRIPTURE

For you know that God paid a ransom to save you from the empty life you inherited from your ancestors. And it was not paid with mere gold or silver, which lose their value. It was the precious blood of Christ, the sinless, spotless Lamb of God (1 Peter 1:18-19).

MEDITATION

"Charity" was a bad word when I was growing up. It was a shame to accept charity. One should always pay for yourself.

Jesus paid for us. The price was high. It cost him his blood. The rate he paid was death on a cross. As the sinless, spotless Lamb of God, it was a debt he did not personally owe.

How do we react to such a gift? Not by wallowing in our unworthiness. Not by trying to pay him back. We respond with gratitude. We say "Thank you" not just with our lips but with our lives. And we joyfully pay debts for our debtors.

"Lamb of God, may we welcome the gift of your death and life."

APRIL 30

HYMN

Will you come, will you come?
How He pleads with you now!
Fly to His loving breast;
And whatever your sin
Or your sorrow may be,
Jesus will give you rest.

SCRIPTURE

So we are Christ's ambassadors; God is making his appeal through us. We speak for Christ when we plead, "Come back to God!" (2 Corinthians 5:20).

MEDITATION

Have you ever begged? Pleaded for a second chance? Craved for more time to pay?

We certainly beg God for forgiveness. What's more amazing is that God, through Jesus, pleads for us to come to him. "Come back to God." "Come, follow me." "I call you by your name."

Do we hear Jesus calling? Pleading? Do we hear him speak in Scripture? Do we catch his words spoken through those around us? Do we understand his voice in the events of the day? How do we listen to that call today? By flying to him. Embracing him. By living worthy of his call.

"Pleading Jesus, may we hear your call."

MAY 1

HYMN

O happy rest! Sweet, happy rest!

Jesus will give you rest.

Oh! Why won't you come

In simple, trusting faith?

Jesus will give you rest.

SCRIPTURE

Then Jesus said, "Come to me, all of you who are weary and carry heavy burdens, and I will give you rest" (Matthew 11:28).

MEDITATION

Who are the most tired people in the world? Perhaps mothers and fathers with newborn babies. They love their child so much, but if only they could get more sleep and rest.

Who rests the most? Perhaps retirees with no work obligations and few family duties. They can sleep late and still nap every day.

But no matter how much sleep and rest you get, there is a deep fatigue that will not go away. The burdens of the past, present, and future overwhelm us. We are weary to our bones.

There is one who promises rest. Will we hear his invitation?

"Lord of rest, take our burdens away."

MAY 2

HYMN

He is coming, the "Man of Sorrows,"
Now exalted on high;

He is coming with loud hosannas,
In the clouds of the sky

SCRIPTURE

Look! He comes with the clouds of heaven. And everyone will see him—even those who pierced him. And all the nations of the world will mourn for him. Yes! Amen! (Revelation 1:7).

MEDITATION

As a kid we always went to the Great Smoky Mountains for our vacation. I remember going around a corner on those twisty mountain roads and seeing a sign, "Jesus is coming soon." What struck me about the sign is that it was incised in stone in the side of a mountain. Which means whoever made the sign didn't expect Jesus to come *too* soon, because he made the sign to last.

After waiting over two thousand years, it's hard to expect Jesus soon. Yet we want him to come and make things right with the world. We want sin and war and death to end. We want every knee to bow to the exalted "Man of Sorrows." Jesus is coming soon!

Today would be a great day for it to happen.

"Lord Jesus, we need you. Come soon and make things right!"

MAY 3

HYMN

He is coming, our loving Savior, / Blessed Lamb that was slain; / In the glory of God the Father, / On the earth He shall reign.

SCRIPTURE

And they sang in a mighty chorus: "Worthy is the Lamb who was slaughtered—to receive power and riches and wisdom and strength and honor and glory and blessing" (Revelation 5:12).

MEDITATION

The Book of Revelation portrays Satan as a large red dragon. It portrays Jesus as a lamb. A dead lamb.

The Main Event. Dragon vs. Dead Lamb. Place your bets.

We know who will win the battle. The powerful always triumph over the vulnerable.

But the Dead Lamb defeats the dragon, throwing him into the bottomless pit (Revelation 20:1-3). God defeats power through weakness. Jesus, the sacrificial Lamb of God, won the battle, has all authority, and will come to reign in glory on the earth.

When we follow that Lamb in sacrificial service, we also trace his steps to glory.

"Lamb of God, may we be your lambs until the day you return."

MAY 4

HYMN

He is coming, our Lord and master,

Our redeemer and king;

We shall see Him in all His beauty,

And His praise we shall sing.

SCRIPTURE

The Son radiates God's own glory and expresses the very character of God, and he sustains everything by the mighty power of his command. When he had cleansed us from our sins, he sat down in the place of honor at the right hand of the majestic God in heaven (Hebrews 1:3).

MEDITATION

God is great. God is good. God also is beauty. I've heard much of God's greatness and goodness, but less of his beauty. Jesus shows the greatness of God in his miracles. He shows the goodness of God in his compassionate healing. Where do we see the beauty of Jesus? I'm not sure Jesus was good-looking, in spite of the Hollywood portrayals. His was the beauty of sacrificial love.

We see that beauty of Jesus today in his followers. We see parents who forfeit their desires for the sake of their children. We see adult children who pour out their lives as caregivers to aged parents. We see those who give themselves in service to neighbors. All through Jesus.

"Beautiful Savior, may we see you today in others."

MAY 5

HYMN

He shall gather His chosen people,
Who are called by His name;
And the ransomed of every nation
For His own He shall claim.

SCRIPTURE

And they sang a new song with these words: "You are worthy to take the scroll and break its Seals and open it. For you were slaughtered, and your blood has ransomed people for God from every tribe and language and people and nation" (Revelation 5:9).

MEDITATION

God has blessed me by allowing me to be with Christians in many countries. In their assemblies I sometimes was the only person there from my country. Sometimes I could not understand a word of their worship.

Except there were two words I understood wherever I was, "Hallelujah" and "Amen."

The day is coming when we praise the Lord with a new song in a language we all can speak. A day when those things that divide us—nation and language and clan—will be swallowed up in our identity in Christ.

May that day come soon! And may we work to see on earth today.

"Lord, open our eyes and ears to all who are called by your Name."

MAY 6

HYMN

Hallelujah! hallelujah!
He is coming again;
And with joy we shall gather round Him,
At His coming to reign.

SCRIPTURE

"Men of Galilee," they said, "why are you standing here staring into heaven? Jesus has been taken from you into heaven, but someday he will return from heaven in the same way you saw him go!" (Acts 1:11).

MEDITATION

Once I was afraid of the Second Coming of Jesus because I did not understand grace. Now I am no longer afraid because I trust he has freely redeemed me. But now I admit I don't often think of his return, perhaps because I have it so good now. It's hard to imagine more joy than the life I have.

Those who know hunger, oppression, and hardship (like Fanny Crosby with her blindness) look forward to the day when those challenges will end, the day Jesus will fully reign. If we begin to grasp the enormity of his grace and gifts, we too will anticipate with joy that glorious appearing. Today would be a good day for his return. Hallelujah! Hallelujah!

"Lord Jesus, come quickly!"

MAY 7

HYMN

Never be afraid to speak for Jesus,

Think how much a word can do;

Never be afraid to own your Savior,

He who loves and cares for you.

SCRIPTURE

One night the Lord spoke to Paul in a vision and told him, "Don't be afraid! Speak out! Don't be silent! For I am with you, and no one will attack and harm you, for many people in this city belong to me" (Acts 18:9-10).

MEDITATION

I am not ashamed of Jesus, but when I meet new people, it takes a while before I tell them I am a Christian.

Why? Because when I do, they begin to treat me differently, unlike a normal person. They start apologizing for their bad words. Or they assume I am condemning them. Or they begin to blame Christians, including me, for all the bad things we have done throughout history. So I keep quiet until I know I can get a fair hearing for what I believe.

At least that's what I tell myself. But perhaps I am afraid to speak for Jesus. I need boldness, not fear, so I might speak for him.

"Lord, let us know that you are with us so we will have courage to speak."

MAY 8

HYMN

Never be afraid to work for Jesus

In His vineyard day by day;

Labor with a kind and willing spirit,

He will all your toil repay.

SCRIPTURE

"At five o'clock that afternoon he was in town again and saw some more people standing around. He asked them, 'Why haven't you been working today?' They replied, 'Because no one hired us.' The landowner told them, 'Then go out and join the others in my vineyard" (Matthew 20:6-7).

MEDITATION

Jesus saves us by his grace, not by our works. We might be afraid to put too much emphasis on working for Jesus because it sounds like "works righteousness."

It can be. We can be proud that we work harder than other Christians and forget the mercy of God is all that saves us. Whether hired at an early or a late hour, we owe the landowner our job.

Yet precisely because we are saved solely by grace, we want to work all the harder. Our works shows our gratitude and love to the one who gave himself for us.

"Jesus, may I never be afraid to work hard for you."

MAY 9

HYMN

Never be afraid to bear for Jesus Patiently endure your every trial,

Keen reproaches when they fall Jesus meekly bore them all.

SCRIPTURE

What blessings await you when people hate you and exclude you and mock you and curse you as evil because you follow the Son of Man (Luke 6:22).

MEDITATION

It is so unfair when others criticize us for doing what is right. Nothing hurts me more.

They did the same to Jesus. They did more than criticize, they put him on a cross. He bore that hurt for us. What's more, he bears the pain we feel when criticized.

Jesus calls us to patience when faced with unjust condemnation. We want to pay back those who insult us with more clever insults. We want to hit back, not turn the other cheek. We do not pay them back because Jesus paid it all, he died for them also. Instead, we pay back evil with good. We follow the one who prayed for the people who put him on that cross. We put up with it, trusting that God will bring justice. We wait. We carry the insults. By the power of Jesus we have the strength and meekness to do so.

"Man of Sorrows, forgive those who sin against us."

MAY
10

HYMN

Never be afraid to die for Jesus,
He the Life, the Truth, the Way,
Gently in His arms of love will bear you
To the realms of endless day.

SCRIPTURE

This is a trustworthy saying: If we die with him, we will also live with him (2 Timothy 2:11).

MEDITATION

Being a martyr is hard to imagine. Although I've had people angry at me because I was a Christian, I can't imagine their violence escalating to murder. But that can happen. I've met families who lost loved ones to violence against Christians.

Yet I do not expect to die for Jesus. The daily martyrdom Jesus expects is enough of a challenge. "Take up your cross daily, and follow me" (Luke 9:23). When we grow tired of being caregivers, when we feel unappreciated, when fellow Christians try our patience, through all the challenges of trusting Jesus, we remember that we are called to die. Death should hold no fear for us, because we have already experienced it. We died in baptism but were raised again (Romans 6:4).

When we die, we die with Jesus. That means we will live in him.

"Gentle Jesus, give us trust in your arms of love even in the face of death."

MAY
11

HYMN

Never be afraid, never be afraid, Jesus is your loving Savior,
Never, never, never; Therefore never be afraid.

SCRIPTURE

So we can say with confidence, "The Lord is my helper, so I will have no fear. What can mere people do to me?" (Hebrews 13:6).

MEDITATION

We live in an age of fear. The media constantly bombards us with stories meant to scare us. I once saw an ad on television that said, "Something in your home may kill you! Watch for details on the evening news." If something might kill us, shouldn't they tell us now? It was just a way to get more eyes on the screen. The danger was not real.

There are enough genuine dangers to frighten us. There are risks in being Christians. We need to be reminded of that when we think all should be blue skies and rainbows when we follow Jesus. We may be afraid to work for Jesus because we think it is in vain. We may be afraid of what others may say when we speak for Jesus. We face fear when we think of dying for Jesus. The clear word from our Savior is, "Do not be afraid."

"Savior, give us trust in you. Take away our fear."

MAY 12

HYMN

Redeemed, how I love to proclaim it!

Redeemed by the blood of the Lamb;

Redeemed through His infinite mercy,

His child, and forever, I am.

SCRIPTURE

Praise the Lord, the God of Israel, because he has visited and redeemed his people (Luke 1:68).

MEDITATION

"Redeem" is a word we don't use much outside of church circles. We do redeem gift certificates and coupons. That is the original meaning of the biblical word redeem, "to buy back" or "to exchange."

Jesus bought us back. We were slaves to sin, slaves to our own unbridled desires. Jesus set us free from that slavery by paying a price. He exchanged his life for ours on the cross. His blood paid for us.

We did not deserve this sacrifice on his part. It is by his infinite grace and mercy. Since he paid a price for us, we now belong to him. We are his children forever.

No wonder we love to proclaim this good news!

"Lamb of God, we joyfully voice our gratitude for our redemption."

MAY
13

HYMN

I think of my blessed Redeemer, I sing, for I cannot be silent;

I think of Him all the day long; His love is the theme of my song.

SCRIPTURE

This great choir sang a wonderful new song in front of the throne of God and before the four living beings and the twenty-four elders. No one could learn this song except the 144,000 who had been redeemed from the earth (Revelation 14:3).

MEDITATION

Christians sing.

But what if you don't like to sing? I know devout Christians who do not enjoy singing.

They sing anyway. Perhaps softly. Perhaps not well. But the joy of redemption causes them to sing.

Singing has a way of uniting what we think and what we feel. When we think of what God has done for us, we cannot help but sing. Even if it is silent singing in our heart.

So sing today with the love of Jesus in your heart.

"Jesus, place your song of love in our minds today."

MAY 14

HYMN

I know I shall see in His beauty
The King in whose law I delight,
Who lovingly guardeth my footsteps,
And giveth me songs in the night.

SCRIPTURE

Your eyes will see the king in his beauty and view a land that stretches afar. (Isaiah 33:17, NIV).

MEDITATION

We rarely describe men, much less kings, as beautiful. We use other words—powerful, majestic, and regal. We don't often refer to God or to Jesus as beautiful. Think of the most beautiful sight you have seen—stately mountains, the waves of the ocean, the most delicate flower. God made them all. He made beauty itself. And while Jesus may not have been physically handsome (in spite of all the Hollywood film portrayals), his beauty shown forth in his sacrificial love for us.

We see the beauty of God in creation and in Jesus, God-made-flesh. But the day will come when we see our King and our Savior face to face. That complete vision of God only comes after our resurrection. The Lord will return, bringing a new heaven and earth. With it he will raise our bodies with new eyes to see clearly what we could not see before, the sight not just of the beauty around us but of the One who is Beauty itself.

"Lord open our eyes to see your beauty this day."

MAY 15

HYMN

Redeemed, redeemed,

Redeemed by the blood of the Lamb;

Redeemed, how I love to proclaim it!

His child, and forever, I am.

SCRIPTURE

Has the Lord redeemed you? Then speak out! Tell others he has redeemed you from your enemies (Psalm 107:2).

MEDITATION

Every child has felt the fear that their parents will abandon them.

One of my earliest memories was being with my mother in a department store. I was walking beside her and suddenly she was gone! I was alone. My mother had deserted me.

Of course, she had done no such thing. I had been distracted by a toy display, taken my eyes off my mother, and she had gone on to the next aisle of the store. When she realized I was not with her she immediately returned. Perhaps she had been gone for a full minute, but it seemed like an hour to me.

Even when we have been walking with Jesus for years, we need reassurance that even when we take our eyes off him, he will never abandon us.

"Jesus, remind us each moment that we are your children forever."

MAY 16

HYMN

Holy Sabbath, day of rest;

By our great Redeemer blest;

When in majesty He rose,

More than conqueror o'er His foes.

SCRIPTURE

Then they went home and prepared spices and ointments to anoint his body. But by the time they were finished the Sabbath had begun, so they rested as required by the law (Luke 23:56).

MEDITATION

Until I'd read these lyrics by Fanny Crosby, I'd never thought of the connection between the death of Jesus and the Sabbath.

Jesus died on Friday and he arose on Sunday. He spent the Sabbath resting in the tomb.

How do we view life after death? Our bodies rest in the grave until Jesus returns and raises them. We then are with the Lord forever in our resurrection bodies. At death, our souls go to be with the Lord. It's not clear what that is like, but it is restful. "Blessed are those who die in the Lord from now on. Yes, says the Spirit, they are blessed indeed, for they will rest from their hard work; for their good deeds follow them!" (Revelation 14:13).

With Jesus, death is a celebration of Sabbath!

"Jesus, thank you for sharing your Sabbath rest with us."

MAY
17

HYMN

Softly now we hear Him say, "Turn from earthly toil away; Let your prayers to Heaven ascend; I will keep you to the end."

SCRIPTURE

Then Jesus said to them, "The Sabbath was made to meet the needs of people, and not people to meet the requirements of the Sabbath" (Mark 2:27).

MEDITATION

"Do we have to keep the Sabbath?"

I've heard dedicated Christians ask that question. It's not a bad question but it can lead to the idea that Sabbath is simply another difficult command from God that we are obligated to keep. We can even argue about when and how to keep the Sabbath. That's what happened in Jesus' day.

We get to keep the Sabbath. It's a blessing, not a burden.

What do we do on the Sabbath? We rest. We sleep. We pray. We worship. For one day a week we trust that God can run the world without us. And if we can do it for one day, we can bring Sabbath into all the other busy days.

"Loving Father, thank you for the gift of Sabbath."

MAY
18

HYMN

Day of worship, hallowed hour,   Give us grace and strength anew,

May the Spirit's quick'ning pow'r   While our journey we pursue.

SCRIPTURE

It was the Lord's Day, and I was worshiping in the Spirit (Revelation 1:10).

MEDITATION

When is the Spirit at work in us?

All the time. At every moment God's Spirit is empowering, encouraging, teaching, and assuring us.

But we get distracted. Sometimes temptation distracts us. Sometimes the work we do, our family obligations, even church activities can cause us to lose our focus on the activity of the Spirit.

Sabbath allows us to be still and listen to the voice of the Spirit. When we worship, we experience the life-giving ("quickening") power of the Spirit. Sabbath reminds us where the strength comes to do our work well, love our families, and serve the world as the people of God.

"Holy Spirit, slow us down so we might know your grace and strength for today."

MAY 19

HYMN

Holy Sabbath, may thy light,   Lift our hearts to God above,

Pure and holy, calm and bright,   Spring of joy, of life, of love.

SCRIPTURE

So there is a special rest still waiting for the people of God (Hebrews 4:9).

MEDITATION

As God's people we are to work hard for him. There is no room for half-hearted effort. So how can we rest? Doesn't rest mean doing nothing?

After six days of creation God rested on the seventh day. So God has done nothing since creation? No way! God has worked to maintain the world. He worked through Abraham, Moses, and Elijah. He became flesh in Jesus who tirelessly served others. He works through the Spirit.

So what does it mean that we share in the "rest" of God? It means we share in His life. "Rest" is the word the Bible uses for all that God has done since creation. It describes God's work as rest.

So through Jesus and the Spirit, our steadfast vigorous work can also be rest. That is Sabbath.

"Creator God, let us enter your rest so we may do your work."

MAY
20

HYMN

Conquering now and still to conquer,

Rideth a king in His might;

Leading the host of all the faithful

Into the midst of the fight.

SCRIPTURE

For the Lord your God is going with you! He will fight for you against your enemies, and he will give you victory! (Deuteronomy 20:4).

MEDITATION

"It's not whether you win or lose, it's how you play the game."

So said the American sportswriter Grantland Rice in 1941.

Like me, most sports fans would say he is wrong. We want our team to win. A close and entertaining game when your team loses is not as fun as a blowout when your team wins. That's even more true when we are talking about a war, not a game. And the war we are talking of is not a battle among nations, but a war between good and evil.

If you read or watch the news, it looks as though the Evil One is winning. But we have the King of Kings leading us into the fight.

"Conquering Jesus, deliver us from evil."

MAY 21

HYMN

Conquering now and still to conquer, Jesus, Thou ruler of all,

Thrones and their scepters all shall perish, Crowns and their splendor shall fall.

SCRIPTURE

I looked up and saw a white horse standing there. Its rider carried a bow, and a crown was placed on his head. He rode out to win many battles and gain the victory (Revelation 6:2).

MEDITATION

Jesus is the Prince of Peace (Isaiah 9:6). At his birth the angels sang, "Glory to God in the highest heaven, and peace on earth to those with whom God is pleased" (Luke 2:14).

Then why is he also the one who rides the white horse into battle, conquering the world? That doesn't sound like peace.

It is peace. But Jesus does not bring peace the way the rulers of the world bring peace. They create peace by violently subduing their enemies. They conquer and rule with an iron fist.

Jesus defeats evil not by a literal sword. He does not redeem by violence. The cross does not display the weak peace of soldiers and arms, but the power of the Almighty. Jesus brings the lasting peace that comes through sacrificial love.

"Prince of Peace, work your powerful conquering love through us."

MAY 22

HYMN

He is our Lord and Redeemer,
Savior and monarch divine;
They are the stars that forever
Bright in His kingdom shall shine.

SCRIPTURE

Live clean, innocent lives as children of God, shining like bright lights in a world full of crooked and perverse people (Philippians 2:15).

MEDITATION

"She's a star." We are used to that language. Actors, singers, athletes, artists, influencers, and even some politicians are stars. So many people are famous today that fame has lost much of its meaning. It doesn't take much to be called a star.

But originally the idea of a star was someone who lighted the path for others. In contrast to the darkness surrounding them, their pure and unselfish lives shone forth clearly.

Such stars shine not with their light but with the glory of God in them. They help others not to gain fame or applause but so others might see God. As Jesus said, "In the same way, let your good deeds shine out for all to see, so that everyone will praise your heavenly Father" (Matthew 6:16).

"Father, may we shine like stars for you today."

MAY 23

HYMN

Not to the strong is the battle,

Not to the swift is the race,

Yet to the true and the faithful

Victory is promised through grace.

SCRIPTURE

The fastest runner doesn't always win the race, and the strongest warrior doesn't always win the battle (Ecclesiastes 9:11).

MEDITATION

"May the best team win."

Another sports cliché that isn't always true. Sometimes the best teams lose badly.

We'd like to think we win the battles of life through our own strength, smarts, and hard work. But sometimes you try your hardest and still lose.

What about the greatest battle of all, the fight against evil? Perhaps you have a besetting sin, one that you have fought all your life but have not been able to overcome. Do you give up? Quit fighting? Do you live in shame and guilt? Do you sin boldly, knowing you cannot win?

None of the above. You trust the grace of the One who gives the victory.

"Jesus, you fought temptation and won. Continue the fight in us."

MAY 24

HYMN

Thou whose hand did lead Thy chosen people

Through the desert on their pilgrim way,

In Thy mercy grant us now Thy blessing,

Jesus help us all to watch and pray.

SCRIPTURE

Remember how the Lord your God led you through the wilderness for these forty years, humbling you and testing you to prove your character, and to find out whether or not you would obey his commands (Deuteronomy 8:2).

MEDITATION

The word for where God led his people can be translated as "wilderness" or "desert."

"Wilderness" always had a good feel for me. It sounds like an adventure in a National Park campground.

"Desert" has a different feel. It reminds me of those classic westerns where the horses die of thirst and the people crawl through the sand with cracked lips. One dries up in the desert. One dies in the desert.

As the Lord led Israel through the desert, so Jesus leads his people through the desert. Our spirits wither and dry without him. We must watch and pray for him to deliver us.

"Jesus, give us the water of life!"

MAY 25

HYMN

Give us water from the sacred fountain,

While we journey in a thirsty land;

Strong in Thee no earthly foe can harm us,

Thou our rock on which we firmly stand.

SCRIPTURE

All of them drank the same spiritual water. For they drank from the spiritual rock that traveled with them, and that rock was Christ (1 Corinthians 10:4).

MEDITATION

Twice God gave the Israelites water from a rock while they were in the desert (Exodus 17:1-6, Numbers 20:2-13). Paul says that rock was Christ, and it followed Israel through the desert.

Paul is not talking of Jesus as a literal traveling rock. He speaks of spiritual water. The loving Father who miraculously provided for Israel has become flesh in Jesus. Jesus gives the living water that quenches all thirst (John 4:10-13).

Jesus also is our rock. We can depend on him. We stand firmly on him. He is the rocky fortress who protects us from all danger.

Trust the rolling rock that travels with us!

"Living Water, flow from us to others today."

MAY 26

HYMN

Gentle Savior, Thou wilt never leave us,

Still from danger and from storm defend,

Sweet the promise to Thy faithful children,

Thou wilt guide and keep them to the end.

SCRIPTURE

For God has said, "I will never fail you. I will never abandon you" (Hebrews 13:5).

MEDITATION

The only true friends are those you can depend on.

We have all experienced the fair-weather friend. They are kind to us when we can do something for them. But when we are in need, they are nowhere to be found. You don't lose when you lose those friends.

But there are friends who are loyal in our times of crisis. They stick with us even when everyone else turns against us. They help us when it costs them greatly.

Our gentle Savior Jesus will never leave our side. It may seem like that at times. But because we believe his sweet promise to never abandon us, we keep our trust in him. He will keep us to the end.

"Dependable Friend, increase our trust in you when danger comes."

MAY
27

HYMN

Though we pass the dark and rolling river,
Thou wilt bear us safely to the shore;
We shall praise Thee in the vales of Eden,
With the saints and angels evermore.

SCRIPTURE

He protects them from the grave, from crossing over the river of death (Job 33:18).

MEDITATION

Twice the Lord led his people safely through a river. He delivered them through the Red Sea as they left Egypt. He led them safely through the desert. He parted the Jordan for them as they entered the promised land.

Many hymns compare death to crossing the Jordan River. As God escorted them through the Jordan to the land he had promised them, so he will guide us safely to the ultimate land of promise—the new heaven and earth.

The verse from Job is the only one in the Bible that makes that comparison between river and death. Yet it is a comforting thought. The power that parted the waters is strong enough to bring us through our fear of death to be forever with our Lord. There we will see his face and praise him forever.

"God of life, usher us safely through death."

MAY
28

HYMN

Father, Thou art pure and holy,

May our hearts Thy temple be,

O, make us humble, meek and lowly,

Poor in spirit, Savior, more like Thee.

SCRIPTURE

Don't you realize that all of you together are the temple of God and that the Spirit of God lives in you? (1 Corinthians 3:16).

MEDITATION

I love visiting the great cathedrals. The soaring arches bring my focus upward toward our Father in heaven. The rainbow colors of the stained glass tell the stories of the love of God in Scripture. I look out at the great space where worshippers throughout the centuries have lifted their voices in song and prayer to God. I think of the centuries of sustained effort it took to build those magnificent edifices.

There is a greater cathedral, a more magnificent temple than any of those great churches. Father, Son, and Spirit now make their home in the human heart. When those hearts are joined together in humble obedience, then the most splendid church arises.

We too are called to the sustained effort to be God's temple.

"Great Builder, make your home in our hearts."

MAY 29

HYMN

To the work! To the work! We are servants of God;

Let us follow the path that our master has trod;

With the balm of His counsel our strength to renew,

Let us do with our might what our hands find to do.

SCRIPTURE

Work willingly at whatever you do, as though you were working for the Lord rather than for people (Colossians 3:23).

MEDITATION

God made work. "The Lord God placed the man in the Garden of Eden to tend and watch over it" (Genesis 2:15). Tending a garden is work, but (like all creation) it was originally good work. God made work as a blessing to humanity.

Then it all went wrong. After the Fall, the ground is cursed and work becomes a burden.

But what we lost in Adam we gain in Christ. Now work again can be a joy and blessing because we are working for the Lord. This does not completely remove the burdensome part of work; every job has its unpleasant tasks, but if we work for the Lord then the Lord works with us, renewing our strength and resolve. As Jesus did the work of his Father, so also we work for God and not people.

"Lord Jesus, give us strength for our work today."

MAY 30

HYMN

To the work! To the work! Let the hungry be fed;

To the fountain of life let the weary be led;

In the cross and its banner our glory shall be,

While we herald the tidings, "Salvation is free!"

SCRIPTURE

Share your food with the hungry, and give shelter to the homeless. Give clothes to those who need them, and do not hide from relatives who need your help (Isaiah 58:7).

MEDITATION

In one of the richest countries in the world, there is hunger. One in twenty families in the U.S.A. report regularly skipping meals or reducing intake because they could not afford more food. The situation in much of the world is much worse.

We may think we do not know anyone who suffers from hunger. We might be surprised that we do. But we need to know them, feed them, and help them. Almost every book in the Bible teaches this. We might disagree on how best to feed the hungry, but as followers of Jesus, we must.

And we should not neglect their deepest hunger, the need for free salvation. We give food and we proclaim the good news.

"Jesus who fed the hungry, open our hearts and hands to do the same."

MAY 31

HYMN

To the work! To the work! There is labor for all;

For the kingdom of darkness and error shall fall;

And the love of our Father exalted shall be,

In the loud swelling chorus, "Salvation is free!"

SCRIPTURE

For he has rescued us from the kingdom of darkness and transferred us into the Kingdom of his dear Son (Colossians 1:13).

MEDITATION

Darkness has always been frightening. We remember the plea from our childhood beds, "Leave the light on."

As adults, we may be less afraid of literal darkness but more afraid of the dark times in which we live. The news always seems so dark—war, poverty, disease, disasters, and crime. If we are not careful, the constant talk of darkness can overwhelm us.

God has left the light on. Through the sacrifice of Jesus, the light of the world shines into the darkness and defeats it. The final word is not the darkness of hate but the exalted love of the Father.

Our work is to let that light shine.

"God of light, may your love shine out of our hearts this day."

JUNE 1

HYMN

To the work! To the work! In the strength of the Lord,

And a robe and a crown shall our labor reward,

When the home of the faithful our dwelling shall be,

And we shout with the ransomed, "Salvation is free!"

SCRIPTURE

For the wages of sin is death, but the free gift of God is eternal life through Christ Jesus our Lord (Romans 6:23).

MEDITATION

We all expect to be paid for our work. There is nothing wrong with that.

But when we think of God rewarding us for our labor, we might think something is not quite right about that. Shouldn't loving our neighbor be its own reward? Should we not do good simply because it is good, not because we want to earn something from God?

Yet even the most enjoyable work becomes tiresome. There is always a point where we do our work because it's our job and we need the pay.

We do not earn salvation. No amount of work can make us right with God. Yet the Lord knows we need a goal to work for, the reward of being with Him forever.

"Lord, may we work hard knowing your gift of salvation is free."

JUNE

2

HYMN

Toiling on, toiling on, Toiling on, toiling on,

Let us hope and trust,

Let us watch and pray,

And labor till the master comes.

SCRIPTURE

Always work enthusiastically for the Lord, for you know that nothing you do for the Lord is ever useless (1 Corinthians 15:58).

MEDITATION

We sang this hymn by Fanny Crosby often in the church of my childhood. It was not one of my favorites, primarily because of this chorus. We sang the hymn so slowly that we truly were "toiling on." I thought the hymn would never end.

Now I appreciate it. Experience has taught me that the best work often becomes toil. We simply must endure. We keep working after the thrill is gone. We work when it seems our work accomplishes little or nothing. We work by faith. We hope. We trust.

We also watch and pray, knowing that it is God who is at work in us. We pray that His will be done. His work is never useless. We watch for his coming when his work in us comes to fruition. Toil on!

"Lord, encourage us in our work for you, that we may labor with enthusiasm."

JUNE 3

HYMN

'Tis not by works that we have done,
Our souls redeemed will be;
But by the blood of God's dear Son,
Who died on Calvary.

SCRIPTURE

He is so rich in kindness and grace that he purchased our freedom with the blood of his Son and forgave our sins (Ephesians 1:7).

MEDITATION

We Americans spend much of our time shopping. We search online for the products with the best reviews. We then compare sellers to get the best price. Some spend hours weekly shopping for groceries, often going to more than one supermarket. And when we find our bargains, we expect what we buy to be as advertised.

The Bible uses purchasing language to describe what God has done for us in Christ. We were no bargain. We came at a high cost. He purchased our freedom with the blood of his Son. Our price was high not because of our intrinsic value. He bought us when we were slaves to sin. But in his eyes, we were worth the price. By grace alone we are his beloved children, his prized possessions.

"God of love, we thank you for purchasing us and making us your own."

JUNE 4

HYMN

'Tis not by works that we can do,
Our righteousness is vain;
But by what Christ Himself hath done,
Eternal life we gain.

SCRIPTURE

For they don't understand God's way of making people right with himself. Refusing to accept God's way, they cling to their own way of getting right with God by trying to keep the law (Romans 10:3).

MEDITATION

I grew up in a church that talked more of works than grace. We believed in grace but not so much in free grace. I remember many sermons on the great day of judgment. On that day, we were told, our sins would be placed on one side of the scale and our good deeds on the other side. If the good deeds weighed more, then heaven. If not, then hell. But if it was close, then God might tip the scales toward heaven by his grace.

Later, when I discovered that salvation was by grace from beginning to end, it was a joyously liberating experience. I appreciate the church that brought me to faith, but I so much wish they had known free grace. That knowledge would have lifted their burden of legalism.

"God of grace, may we rely on the blood of Jesus alone for our salvation."

JUNE 5

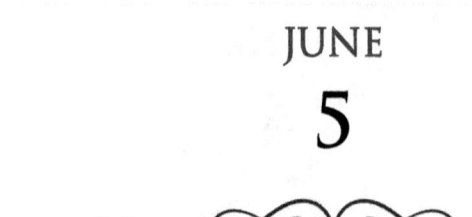

HYMN

'Tis not by works of ours that we
Can know our sins forgiv'n;
But by the living word of Him
Who pleads for us in Heav'n.

SCRIPTURE

Who then will condemn us? No one—for Christ Jesus died for us and was raised to life for us, and he is sitting in the place of honor at God's right hand, pleading for us (Romans 8:34).

MEDITATION

The leaders in that legalistic church of my youth decided to interview each member to see where they stood spiritually. To do that they asked each one, "If you died tonight, would you go to heaven?"

Some answered "No." That led to some pastoral intervention. The majority answered, "I hope so." They were not sure they had done enough good work to qualify. Some answered, "Yes." That led to the follow-up question, "How can you be sure?" Most answered by listing all the good things they had done.

But one woman answered, "I know I'm going to heaven because Jesus told me so."

She understood grace and faith.

"Jesus, increase our trust in your word of salvation."

JUNE 6

HYMN

'Tis not our works, but Christ's alone,
Then rest thy anxious soul;
For safe thou art on Him, thy rock,
While endless ages roll.

SCRIPTURE

He alone is my rock and my salvation, my fortress where I will never be shaken (Psalm 62:2).

MEDITATION

Rock stands for strength. A professional wrestler who calls himself "The Rock" wants everyone to know he is the strongest. Rock also stands for dependable. A financial services company once urged people to "own a piece of the rock." It was their way of saying their investments were sound. Rock can stand for invulnerable. You cannot escape from a prison known as "The Rock." A rock fortress cannot be breached.

When we worry that we are not strong enough, when we need a dependable shelter, we turn to the Rock of Ages. The Evil One cannot overcome us because Jesus is stronger. He defeated Satan on the cross and the empty tomb. Our doubts cannot overwhelm us because our trust is as sure as the Rock. Since we depend on Christ alone, our salvation is sure, whatever may happen.

"Jesus, we rest in you as our rock and fortress."

JUNE 7

HYMN

By grace are ye saved, And that not of yourselves,

By grace are ye saved thro' faith, It is the gift of God.

SCRIPTURE

God saved you by his grace when you believed. And you can't take credit for this; it is a gift from God. Salvation is not a reward for the good things we have done, so none of us can boast about it (Ephesians 2:8-9).

MEDITATION

We are saved by free grace. We did nothing to deserve it.

So why are there so many hymns and Bible verses on good works? If our good works cannot save us, why do them?

Sequence is important here. If we do good works thinking they will earn a reward from God, we deceive ourselves. That way only leads either to pride or despair.

But if we trust Jesus when he says he died for us, that all our sins (past, present, and future) are forgiven, then we are confident of our relationship with God. We are his beloved children. Because we know he loves us, we want to please him. Grace produces good works.

"God of grace, give us grace to love you and love our neighbors today."

HYMN

I am Thine, O Lord, I have heard Thy voice,

And it told Thy love to me;

But I long to rise in the arms of faith

And be closer drawn to Thee.

SCRIPTURE

Let us go right into the presence of God with sincere hearts fully trusting him (Hebrews 10:22).

MEDITATION

How do we know we are growing closer to God? Is it based on feeling? But we have little control of our feelings. Do we know we are closer because we sin less? Yet it seems like we struggle with sin as much or more than we used to. Are we loving God and our neighbor more? How would we measure that?

Perhaps the question should be, "Do we want to be closer to God?" Is it a deep longing or have we become complacent in our walk with the Lord?

The answer is that we know we are growing closer to the Lord by faith. We trust that our desire to grow closer to Jesus is shown by small acts, like daily devotional time, and that Jesus blesses those small acts. We trust that the desire to please God, even if we do not always act on that desire, is itself pleasing to God.

"Lord Jesus, draw us closer to you this day."

JUNE 9

HYMN

Consecrate me now to Thy service, Lord,

By the power of grace divine;

Let my soul look up with a steadfast hope,

And my will be lost in Thine.

SCRIPTURE

Do not let any part of your body become an instrument of evil to serve sin. Instead, give yourselves completely to God, for you were dead, but now you have a new life. So use your whole body as an instrument to do what is right for the glory of God (Romans 6:13).

MEDITATION

"Consecrate" is a thoroughly religious word. It means to be completely devoted to God. It's the word used to describe those who have taken lifetime vows to serve God.

Which means us. It is not only those who take special orders who have made vows to God. Baptism is a vow of service and obedience. We pledged ourselves in baptism to be loyal to the Father, Son, and Spirit. We have been consecrated to God.

How can we fulfill such a vow? Not by our own efforts alone. Only by the power of the Holy Spirit in us, the power of grace, can we hold on to our hope. Only by that power can we be holy—consecrated to the Lord.

"God of grace, make us holy this day through your Holy Spirit."

JUNE 10

HYMN

O the pure delight of a single hour
That before Thy throne I spend,
When I kneel in prayer, and with Thee, my God
I commune as friend with friend!

SCRIPTURE

Inside the Tent of Meeting, the Lord would speak to Moses face to face, as one speaks to a friend (Exodus 33:11).

MEDITATION

To speak to God as a friend seems too intimate a relationship with the Almighty. He is God and we are not.

Yet what Moses and a few other experienced is now promised to all who trust in Jesus. We can enter the very throne room of God. We can unburden our hearts to our Father as we would to our closest friend. And God wants to listen to us! He wants to dialogue with us. He wants to comfort and protect. He is the friend on whom we can always depend.

This does not mean we are equal to God. We come on bent knee, acknowledging him as the King of the Universe. Yet the King is our friend. Can we not make the time to spend an hour with that friend?

"God of love, may I delight in my time with you."

JUNE 11

HYMN

There are depths of love that I cannot know

Till I cross the narrow sea;

There are heights of joy that I may not reach

Till I rest in peace with Thee.

SCRIPTURE

So there is a special rest still waiting for the people of God (Hebrews 4:9).

MEDITATION

R.I.P. Rest in peace. You see it on old tombstones.

When we die in the Lord, we do enter into his rest and peace. To some that may sound like nothing happens. That's why many think they will be bored in heaven throughout eternity.

But the rest God promises is an active rest. Being with the Lord is never static or boring. He is the source of all novelty and pleasure. So in the new heaven and earth he promises there will be change and growth. There will be deeper love and higher joys.

So we look forward to the time when our worn out mortal bodies are made immortal, the time when we see Jesus with new eyes. Then there will be a rest and peace that we cannot fathom.

"Lord, remove our fear of death and make us anxious for your peace and rest."

JUNE 12

HYMN

Draw me nearer, nearer blessed Lord,

To the cross where Thou hast died.

Draw me nearer, nearer, nearer blessed Lord,

To Thy precious, bleeding side.

SCRIPTURE

I want to know Christ and experience the mighty power that raised him from the dead. I want to suffer with him, sharing in his death (Philippians 3:10).

MEDITATION

We want to draw nearer to God because that closeness promises rest, peace, and joy.

But the path to glory always goes through the cross. If we desire joys beyond description, we must also want to know suffering with Christ.

This can be misunderstood. We Christians do not enjoy suffering. The greatest Christian is not the one who is most miserable and who spreads that misery to others. What we announce is good news, not a promise of more pain. Yet Jesus calls us to die with him, to take up our cross, because he knows that new life follows death. The bleeding side brings healing.

"Jesus, draw us through your cross to life everlasting."

JUNE 13

HYMN

Let us mingle our voices in chorus today;

The earth is rejoicing, all nature is gay,

And the stream in the valley goes laughing along;

How happy its beautiful song.

SCRIPTURE

Let the heavens be glad, and the earth rejoice! Let the sea and everything in it shout his praise! (Psalm 96:11).

MEDITATION

This is one of the many hymns that Fanny Crosby wrote for children. As adults, we may feel its sentimentality and simplicity are too childish for us.

But Jesus told us to be like children. We need to recapture the wonder we felt as children when we first saw a babbling brook or the clear blue sky. The Bible often uses simple, even sentimental language to speak of the creation praising its Creator. The beauty that surrounds us sings a song of joy to the God who made beauty and joy.

This is also how the Bible speaks of the new heaven and earth to come. There will be the river of life and the trees of life, a delightful garden, a paradise where we will be with the Lord forever. Let us, like children, catch a glimpse of it now.

"Creator God, you made all things beautiful. Open our eyes to that splendor."

JUNE 14

HYMN

There is joy in the sunbeam that sparkles so bright

And calls the young blossoms to welcome the light;

And the bird in the greenwood is singing with glee,

As cheerful and happy as we.

SCRIPTURE

The flowers are springing up, the season of singing birds has come, and the cooing of turtledoves fills the air (Song of Solomon 2:12).

MEDITATION

Spring has come to where I live and with it the return of the birds. We have birds all year, but a greater variety comes in the Spring.

I love birds. I'm not one of those "birders" who spend their days looking for a new species to check off their list. I don't even know what some of the birds I see are called. Yet I can spend hours on my back porch, watching the variety of shapes and colors that fly past me. I listen for a variety of song. There are over 50 billion birds in the world, each bringing joy and cheer to those who are willing to sit and watch and listen.

Then there are the flowers with all their variations of shape and color.

If we want to see God, we only need to open our eyes.

"Beautiful God, cheer our day through the sights that surround us."

JUNE 15

HYMN

Let us join the glad music and joyfully raise,

In purest devotion, our jubilant praise;

We are grateful to God for this beautiful day:

We'll sing the bright moments away.

SCRIPTURE

"You alone are the Lord. You made the skies and the heavens and all the stars. You made the earth and the seas and everything in them. You preserve them all, and the angels of heaven worship you" (Nehemiah 9:6).

MEDITATION

Why does God want our praise? Is he a needly God who would be impoverished without our words of affirmation?

No. God needs nothing from us.

Yet God wants something from us. He wants all of us. If we have a relationship with God by his grace, then we cannot help but be thankful. We cannot keep from praise. We must break out in joyful song.

When we see a gorgeous sunset, we cannot suppress a "Wow!" We call it "glorious" because it expresses the ultimate Glory.

"God of glory, we praise you, we thank you, we rejoice in you."

JUNE 16

HYMN

Praise the Lord, the giver of all,
Praise the Lord, the giver of all;
Let His children with rapture His mercy recall,
The bountiful giver of all.

SCRIPTURE

Teach those who are rich in this world not to be proud and not to trust in their money, which is so unreliable. Their trust should be in God, who richly gives us all we need for our enjoyment (1 Timothy 6:17).

MEDITATION

Everyone wants to win the billion-dollar lottery. Then we would have it made. We'd have nothing to worry about.

But a billion dollars is less than what God promises. He owns all the billions in the world.

And he's decided to give it away! What he gives is more reliable than money. He freely gives us everything we need for our enjoyment.

Who says we can't have it all? God gives all. He asks us to turn away from the false promise of riches to turn to the source of all good gifts. The best things in life are free. The best of all is free—a God who loves us infinitely.

"God of love, turn us from false values to find you—the Giver of all."

JUNE 17

HYMN

Have you sought for the sheep that have wandered,
Far away on the dark mountains cold?

Have you gone, like the tender Shepherd,
To bring them again to the fold?

SCRIPTURE

If a man has a hundred sheep and one of them gets lost, what will he do? Won't he leave the ninety-nine others in the wilderness and go to search for the one that is lost until he finds it? (Matthew 15:4).

MEDITATION

"Acceptable losses."

It's a phrase used in warfare and in business. If an army wins a battle with 1% losses, it's considered a great victory. If a business loses only 1% in waste or theft, it considers that good.

No loss is acceptable to Jesus. He leaves the ninety-nine to find the one. If we follow Jesus, we too must not see the loss of a single person as "acceptable." Instead, we search for those who are lost in every sense of that word. They cannot find their way in life. They need someone to gently guide, to walk beside them in their struggles. We bring them safely into the fold of the Great Shepherd who loves them.

"Great Shepherd, give us a heart for those who cannot find their way in life."

JUNE 18

HYMN

Have you followed their weary footsteps?

And the wild desert waste have you crossed,

Nor lingered till safe home returning,

You have gathered the sheep that were lost?

SCRIPTURE

For the Son of Man came to seek and save those who are lost (Luke 19:10).

MEDITATION

Even with GPS we can get lost.

It happens to me when visiting a new city. Even with my map program in my hand, I end up going in the wrong direction. Eventually I find the way the arrow points. But I've lost time.

We all know the feeling of being lost.

Churches sometimes speak of "the lost" as if they are completely to blame for their lack of direction on life. They should know better (like we do)! But when life falls apart and everything is disoriented, we need help, not judgment. So we must give that help to others. We do not wait for them to get their act together or even for them to ask for help. We search for them. We bring them safely home.

"Lord Jesus, may we, like you, seek and save the lost."

JUNE 19

HYMN

Have you been to the sad and the lonely,

Whose burdens are heavy to bear?

Have you carried the name of Jesus,

And tenderly breathed it in prayer?

SCRIPTURE

Share each other's burdens, and in this way obey the law of Christ (Galatians 6:2).

MEDITATION

Unless you move furniture for a living then you probably do not carry heavy loads.

But we do. The invisible loads weigh us down more than the visible ones. Money worries, health scares, and family troubles burden us. They sometimes make us physically stoop under their weight. We can no longer lift our heads. Our shoulders ache.

Then there are the heavier loads of shame and guilt we carry.

We need someone to share the load. Jesus carries it with us. That's why his yoke is easy, and his burden is light. But we are also called to share the burdens of others. We take the load off their shoulders by helping them financially, assisting their family, and giving a kind word. We also lift them up in prayer to the great Lifter of Loads.

"Broad-Shouldered Jesus, carry our load and those of others this day."

JUNE 20

HYMN

Have you told of the great salvation

He died on the cross to secure?

Have you asked them to trust in the Savior,

Whose love shall forever endure?

SCRIPTURE

So what makes us think we can escape if we ignore this great salvation that was first announced by the Lord Jesus himself and then delivered to us by those who heard him speak? (Hebrews 2:3).

MEDITATION

Some churches have an unofficial "catch and release" program when it comes to saving people. We get them into the waters of baptism and then into church for a while, but then we ignore their genuine needs. Jesus not only saved souls, he healed the sick and fed the hungry. We also meet the needs of our neighbors.

And their deepest need is for the full salvation that Jesus promises. Yes, he healed the sick, but he also told them, "Your sins are forgiven." Yes, he fed the hungry, but he urges them to hunger for the Bread of Life.

"Great Physician, Bread of Life, may we lead others to trust your full salvation."

JUNE 21

HYMN

Have you knelt by the sick and the dying,

The message of mercy to tell?

Have you stood by the trembling captive

Alone in his dark prison cell?

SCRIPTURE

I was naked, and you gave me clothing. I was sick, and you cared for me. I was in prison, and you visited me (Matthew 25:36).

MEDITATION

Prisons are terrible places. I don't want to go there. In the first century, prisons were even worse than they are today. Usually, they were a pit, a hole in the ground, or a dungeon. They usually did not feed you in prison. If you starve, so be it.

So to visit someone in prison meant more than a short call to cheer someone. It means bringing them food and warm clothing so they could stay alive.

As God's people we must visit prisons. But we must do more. We must help prisoners when they need it most, immediately after release. At the halfway house we can teach them skills, get them jobs, keep them from substance abuse, and be their friends. This is a true visit. We can even lead them to the one who promised release to the captives.

"God of love, stand beside prisoners. May we stand with them."

JUNE 22

HYMN

Have you pointed the lost to Jesus,

And urged them on Him to believe?

Have you told of the life everlasting,

That all, if they will, may receive?

SCRIPTURE

For this is how God loved the world: He gave his one and only Son, so that everyone who believes in him will not perish but have eternal life (John 3:16).

MEDITATION

Fanny Crosby spent much of her life helping others in the Rescue Missions of New York City. She not only wrote hymns about helping the needy, but she also came to their aid.

But that's not all she did. Through her hymns, her words, and her deeds, she also proclaimed the Good News of Jesus and urged others to make him their Savior.

For more than a century, Christians in America were divided into two camps. One followed the social gospel that focused on meeting physical needs and fighting injustice. The other emphasized "saving souls," sometimes at the expense of meeting bodily needs. In the past few decades, both sides have embraced a more unified gospel that cares for body and soul. Fanny Crosby pioneered that approach.

"Lord of body and spirit, may we fight for justice and urge others to believe."

JUNE 23

HYMN

If to Jesus you answer these questions,
And to Him have been faithful and true,

Then behold, in the mansions yonder
Are crowns of rejoicing for you;

SCRIPTURE

"The master was full of praise. 'Well done, my good and faithful servant. You have been faithful in handling this small amount, so now I will give you many more responsibilities. Let's celebrate together!'" (Matthew 25:21).

MEDITATION

We have all spent time, money, and effort helping others and receiving nothing in return, not even a word of thanks. Sometimes those we try to help even turn on us and take advantage of our good nature. It seems that we are being punished for our good deeds.

Even if all that is true, we still generously give our time, money, and effort. We give out of gratitude to God for all he has done for us. And we give, trusting that God will reward us for what we have done. We may sow in sorrow, but we reap in joy. As Jesus was faithful to his calling, even though it led to the cross, so we take up the cross of service in confidence that it will end in resurrection and glory.

"Faithful Jesus, make us faithful in our service to you and to our neighbors."

JUNE 24

HYMN

And there from the King eternal
Your welcome and greeting shall be,

"Inasmuch as 'twas done for My brethren,
Even so it was done unto Me."

SCRIPTURE

"And the King will say, 'I tell you the truth, when you did it to one of the least of these my brothers and sisters, you were doing it to me!'" (Matthew 25:40).

MEDITATION

In the parable in Matthew 25, we are judged by how we serve the hungry, thirsty, imprisoned, and naked. Those who did not serve them are astounded that the King says they did not serve him. Those who care for the needy find they have cared for the King.

How do we look at those who need our help? Are they a bother? Do we ignore them? They come to our churches, stand on our street corners, and constantly ask for more. Are we burned out from helping them?

What if we saw Jesus begging at the church door or on the corner? Would we stop and help him? If we can see Jesus in the faces of those who are ever present and wanting help, then we do not grow tired of doing good.

"Great King, may we see you this day in those who need our help."

JUNE 25

HYMN

No book is like the Bible, / For childhood, youth and age; / Our duty, plain and simple, / We find on every page.

SCRIPTURE

You have been taught the holy Scriptures from childhood, and they have given you the wisdom to receive the salvation that comes by trusting in Christ Jesus (2 Timothy 3:15).

MEDITATION

I've always been skeptical of hymns that praise the Bible. Many sound as if the Bible itself saves us. However, Crosby's hymn rightly emphasizes the message of the Bible that saves.

Knowing the Scriptures from childhood is a great gift. This is not about pride in knowing more Bible than others. Instead, through the Bible the Spirit opens our hearts to hear a word from God. The Scriptures give us the wisdom to put our trust in Jesus.

Studying and meditation on the Bible is not for children alone. We rightfully teach our children at home and send them to Sunday School to learn the Bible. Perhaps the best thing we can do for our children is to spend time meditating on the word of God for ourselves. We cannot give what we do not have—a saving knowledge of the Scriptures.

"God who speaks, open the ears of our hearts to listen."

JUNE 26

HYMN

It came by inspiration,   A voice from Him who gave it,

A light to guide our way,   Reproving when we stray.

SCRIPTURE

All Scripture is inspired by God and is useful to teach us what is true and to make us realize what is wrong in our lives. It corrects us when we are wrong and teaches us to do what is right (2 Timothy 3:16).

MEDITATION

Like Timothy, many of us have known the Scriptures since childhood. Why do we continue to study our Bibles? Perhaps out of obligation. We should indeed study the Bible. Maybe out of habit. There's nothing wrong with that. Reading the Bible daily is a good habit. Yet we should expect God to do something through the Scriptures. By reading and meditating on the Bible, God shapes us into the image of Jesus, through the Holy Spirit. This is more than simply an intellectual study. The Bible gives us strength and guidance to overcome an evil culture with good. "God uses it to prepare and equip his people to do every good work" (2 Timothy 3:17).

The habit of Bible study changes us profoundly.

"God of power, give us power through your word to do your will today."

JUNE 27

HYMN

No book is like the Bible,   The pilgrim's chart of glory,

The blessed book we love,   It leads to God above.

SCRIPTURE

I have obeyed your laws, for I love them very much (Psalm 119:167).

MEDITATION

"Law." The word does not warm my heart. Law sounds like rules, regulations, and red tape. How can one love law unless one is a legalistic rule-keeper?

The Hebrew word, usually translated "law," is *torah*. A better translation of the word is "instruction." That has a different feel. We think of a stern father or mother who lays down the law. On the other hand, a loving parent provides gentle instruction to their child.

God is a loving Father who does not leave his children to figure out life on their own. He patiently instructs them how to live so they will have genuine joy in life. God shows us how to love him and to love our neighbors.

So it is right for us to say, "I love the Bible." We love it because it leads us to the God we love. We are thankful for our Father's instruction.

"Loving Father, may we obey your instruction to us so we may live."

HYMN

It tells of man's creation, / His sad, primeval fall; / It tells of man's redemption, / Through Christ, who died for all.

SCRIPTURE

Yes, Adam's one sin brings condemnation for everyone, but Christ's one act of righteousness brings a right relationship with God and new life for everyone (Romans 5:18).

MEDITATION

Here is the story of the Bible.

God made all things good. Adam and Eve chose to do things their way. They disobey God. Sin enters the world and with it decay and death. Sin gets worse. The first sin in the Bible is eating forbidden fruit. The second is the murder of a brother.

In his mercy, God calls a man, Abraham, and through that man calls a nation, Israel. From that nation that is loyal to him, God sends his own Son, Jesus. Jesus redeems humanity on the cross. He defeats sin and death on the cross and at the empty tomb. Jesus will come again to bring a new heaven and earth.

What we lost in Adam, we gain in Jesus. And much more.

"God of Creation and New Creation, remind us always of this wonderful story."

JUNE 29

HYMN

in sacred words of wisdom
It bids us watch and pray,
And early come to Jesus,
The Life, the Truth, the Way.

SCRIPTURE

"You search the Scriptures because you think they give you eternal life. But the Scriptures point to me!" (John 5:39).

MEDITATION

Imagine you have built your dream house in the Rocky Mountains. One wall of that house is a huge window. Through it you see the majestic beauty of the mountains.

Then you notice a smudge on the window. Then another. You spend your time cleaning the window, making it spotless. You spend so much time cleaning it that you forget what a window is for.

Some spend a lot of time studying their Bibles, arguing over the smallest points. But they forget what the Bible is for. Like a window, we look through Scripture to see the beauty of Jesus. Bible study is never an end in itself. The Bible itself does not save. It reveals the One who saves. We see the Giver of life in its pages.

"Savior, may we see you in our Bible study this day."

JUNE 30

HYMN

Love God, our Lord and Savior,
Who reigns in Heaven above,
And bids us all remember,
Our neighbors we must love

SCRIPTURE

Jesus replied, "'You must love the Lord your God with all your heart, all your soul, and all your mind.' This is the first and greatest commandment" (Matthew 22:37-38).

MEDITATION

Do I love the Lord my God?

Of course, I do. He made me, saved me, and blesses me beyond description.

Do I love the Lord my God with all my heart, soul, and mind?

That I'm not so sure of. My heart gives itself to many things. My soul or self is divided among several pursuits. And my mind flits all over the place. Like Israel of old, I pledge to serve the Lord alone and then find myself distracted by other goods and other gods.

I don't think I'm alone. Many Christians feel this way. We are Christians but bad Christians who cannot always focus on God alone. The Lord understands.

"God of love, through your Spirit increase our love for you."

JULY 1

HYMN

For on these great commandments
To Christians here below
Hang all the law and prophets;
The Bible tells us so.

SCRIPTURE

"A second is equally important: 'Love your neighbor as yourself.' The entire law and all the demands of the prophets are based on these two commandments" (Matthew 22:39-40).

MEDITATION

If I have trouble loving God, I have more trouble loving my neighbors.

Have you met my neighbors? They're loud, selfish, and a pain to be around. It seems easy to love God who gave his Son for us. We love Jesus who died for us and now intercedes for us. It is harder to love the flesh-and-blood neighbor we see every day.

Our love for neighbor does not come naturally from their niceness. That love comes from God's love for us and God's love for them. It is not natural but supernatural, one of the fruits of the Spirit. If we are not sure we love God with all our heart, soul, and mind, the great test is "Do I treat others the way I want to be treated?" By God's power, we can. Jesus says these are all the commands we need.

"Lord God, give us the power to keep these two great commands."

JULY 2

HYMN

Thy Holy Spirit, Lord, alone, / Can turn our hearts from sin; / His power alone can sanctify / And keep us pure within.

SCRIPTURE

God the Father knew you and chose you long ago, and his Spirit has made you holy. As a result, you have obeyed him and have been cleansed by the blood of Jesus Christ (1 Peter 1:2).

MEDITATION

We must work hard for Jesus. We are called to do our best. We should show compassion to our neighbors. We flee temptation and overcome sin.

Who can do all these things? Not me. I struggle to love my neighbor. I don't do enough to serve God. My heart is not in what little I do. I fight against sin sometimes, but there are temptations I give into over and over. I cannot be good enough.

Am I alone? Or do you feel this way too? Is there hope for us? Who can help?

The Holy Spirit of God lives in us. We are not in this struggle alone. We trust that he makes us holy, gives us strength to love, and turns our hearts from sin.

"Holy God, make us holy this day through the power of the Spirit."

JULY 3

HYMN

Thy Holy Spirit, Lord, alone
Can deeper love inspire;
His power alone within our souls
Can light the sacred fire.

SCRIPTURE

For we know how dearly God loves us, because he has given us the Holy Spirit to fill our hearts with his love (Romans 5:5).

MEDITATION

It is hard to love some people.

You know who they are. They are always critical, always complaining, and never satisfied. Others are hard to love because they require so much time and effort to help. Caregiving can drain us no matter how much we love someone. We get to the point where we have no more strength to love.

Christian love for neighbor is not based on the lovability of others. We do not love them because they love us. Of course, when they do love us, it makes it easier to love them. But Christian love is supernatural. It comes from God through the Holy Spirit. When we think we cannot last another day in caring for others, the Spirit lights the fire of love.

"Spirit of Love, give us strength and patience to love the unlovable."

JULY 4

HYMN

Thy Holy Spirit, Lord, can bring
The gifts we seek in prayer;
His voice can words of comfort speak,
And still each wave of care.

SCRIPTURE

And the Holy Spirit helps us in our weakness. For example, we don't know what God wants us to pray for. But the Holy Spirit prays for us with groanings that cannot be expressed in words (Romans 8:26).

MEDITATION

For years people have come to me with their struggles. They face horrible home situations, financial woes, addictive behavior, and painful sickness. I often can be of little help to them. Many times, I don't even know what can help them. Their challenges seem beyond solution.

What I have done is pray for them. Even then, I often don't know what to pray for. The good news is that we don't have to know what is best for others to pray for them. We can trust that God knows what they need better than we know. And the Spirit can take our genuine concern for them and turn our inarticulate groanings into a request that the Lord will bless.

"Spirit who knows what is best, help us when we pray."

JULY 5

HYMN

Thy Holy Spirit, Lord, can give
The grace we need this hour;

And while we wait, O Spirit, come
In sanctifying power.

SCRIPTURE

May the grace of the Lord Jesus Christ, the love of God, and the fellowship of the Holy Spirit be with you all (2 Corinthians 13:14).

MEDITATION

"Take it one day at a time."

We have all heard that good advice. But it is much easier said than done. The cares of life threaten to overwhelm us. We feel as if we cannot stand what we face another hour, much less a day. We need help now!

Often when we desperately need help from the Lord, he tells us to wait. I do not like to wait. But waiting is the only way we learn patience.

The Holy Spirit gives us the power to wait on the Lord. We know the Spirit has helped us in the past. We trust that he is helping us now, even when we cannot see that help. The Spirit will help us this hour, this day. He will come with power.

"Lord God, give us your Spirit so we may wait for you."

JULY 6

HYMN

As the bird flies home to its parent nest,

When the hunter seeks his prey,

O child of God, to thy Father haste,

From the tempter's snare away.

SCRIPTURE

We escaped like a bird from a hunter's trap. The trap is broken, and we are free! (Psalm 124:7).

MEDITATION

Have you ever been a target? Others are out to get you. They lay in wait to trap you. No matter what you do or what you say, you cannot escape their plots against you.

It's not always paranoia when you think everyone is against you.

Who can protect us from those out to get us? Who can shield us from our ultimate enemy who constantly schemes to turn us from happiness?

"Deliver us from evil," we pray. And God hears. He rescues us from Satan, the evil one. He shelters us from others who mean us harm. He sets us free from all that threatens to snare us. We are free from worry, from danger, from sickness, from poverty, from injustice, and from violence. We rest safely in the nest of God.

"Our Father, protect us from all evil this day."

JULY 7

HYMN

When the winds are cold, and the days are long,

And thy soul from care would hide,

Fly back, fly back, to thy Father then,

And beneath His wings abide.

SCRIPTURE

He will cover you with his feathers. He will shelter you with his wings. His faithful promises are your armor and protection (Psalm 91:4).

MEDITATION

Spring has come and gone and with it the spectacle of new life. The birds take time to build their nests twig by twig. Mothers sit on eggs, patiently waiting for them to hatch. The first beaks peak out from the shells and soon we hear the shrill cries of the babies. Mother and father take turns constantly feeding the nestlings. They protect that nest from predators and other birds.

It's an interesting picture of Almighty God. Like these birds, he prepares a home for us. He feeds us. He protects us. God is the momma bird who gently shields us beneath her wings.

No matter how adult and independent we are, there are times when we need to be mothered—the Lord mothers and fathers us. We rest in complete safety from the cold, long days in the shelter of his wings.

"Mother God, fold us safe in your arms, under your wings."

JULY 8

HYMN

Oh, the tranquil joy of that dear retreat,

Where the Savior bids thee rest,

With steadfast hope, and a trusting faith,

In His love secure and blest.

SCRIPTURE

Then Jesus said, "Come to me, all of you who are weary and carry heavy burdens, and I will give you rest" (Matthew 11:28).

MEDITATION

Like you, I have been on several spiritual retreats. Most of the ones I attended were overly scheduled. They seemed more like a course or seminar and less like a restful retreat.

Retreats that are genuinely restful are of great value. They allow us to focus on what is most important in our hectic lives. But the retreat and rest Jesus promises is more than a weekend every few months or years. He calls us to rest amid our busyness and clutter.

Practicing a regular Sabbath or taking a retreat trains our minds and hearts to rest in God at all times. They remind us that God is in control. They increase our capacity for hope and trust. They allow us to constantly rest in the assurance that we are God's beloved children, no matter how much or how little we accomplish. All by his grace.

"Jesus, we come to you with our heavy burdens, asking for your rest."

JULY 9

HYMN

'Tis the Lord thy God that to thee has said,

He will guide thee with His eye;

In all thy need, like the weary dove,

To Thy only refuge fly.

SCRIPTURE

But let all who take refuge in you rejoice; let them sing joyful praises forever. Spread your protection over them, that all who love your name may be filled with joy (Psalm 5:11).

MEDITATION

Refugee.

The word has a particular flavor in our culture. Refugees have fled from oppressive situations to find a better place to live. Sometimes they flee because they and those they love can no longer live at all in their homeland. Refugees are powerless. They depend on the help and goodwill of those in their adopted country.

Many localities do not want refugees. They see them as burdens, disrupting the economy and society.

All Christians are refugees. We have fled the culture we live in, no matter how good it may seem, to take refuge in the Lord. He welcomes us with open arms.

"God of the downtrodden, we desperately come to you for refuge."

JULY 10

HYMN

Under His wings thy defense shall be,

He with His feathers shall cover thee,

Cover thee, cover thee,

He with His feathers will cover thee.

SCRIPTURE

How precious is your unfailing love, O God! All humanity finds shelter in the shadow of your wings (Psalm 36:7).

MEDITATION

I was young and inexperienced when I started my first teaching job. Betty Bates was my boss. But more than that, she was a seasoned teacher who took me under her wing. She protected me from the (perhaps just) criticism from my students and their parents. She covered for me.

"They took me under their wing." It's the phrase we use for someone who taught us the ropes and sheltered us from pitfalls. "I've got you covered." It's what we say when others defend us or pay the way for us.

The Lord God has taken us under his wing. No matter what happens he has our back. He shields us from harm. He shows us how to live in a world that often baffles us with its complexity. No matter what, he covers us.

"Loving God, may we depend on your guidance and protection. Thank you for the cover."

JULY 11

HYMN

"O serve the Lord with gladness,"   He is the great Creator,

And come before His throne;   And He is God alone;

SCRIPTURE

Worship the Lord with gladness. Come before him, singing with joy (Psalm 100:2).

MEDITATION

I have known some sour Christians in my time. If they were filled with the joy of the Lord, they hid it well.

I have also known Christians who were happy and cheerful all day long. At least they seemed that way. One soon found they were profoundly troubled and just putting on a good front.

Christian joy or gladness can be misunderstood. It is not a shallow optimism that all is well. Instead it is that deep joy that comes from hope, a gladness stemming from trust in the Creator.

If God is God, then he has made all things good. They went bad, but through Jesus he is recreating a world of gladness.

"Loving God, give us your deep joy and gladness this day."

HYMN

The heavens declare His glory, / The earth His power displays; / While millions without number / To Him glad anthems raise.

SCRIPTURE

The heavens proclaim the glory of God. The skies display his craftsmanship (Psalm 19:1).

MEDITATION

It is a joy to admire a beautiful painting or listen to a moving symphony. Our joy is in the painting and the music itself but also in the thought that a human being created this. As one who cannot draw or compose, I am in awe of what others can do.

It is a joy to view the created world, to hear the songs of birds and frogs, to smell the flowers. The joy is in experiencing their beauty but also in the thought that only God made all this. Overwhelmed with that joy we cannot help but break out in song.

We are glad when we encounter the beauty of creation. Yet that joy pales beside the delight when we humbly come before the throne of God in prayer. Our hearts erupt in song and praise before the only true God.

Come to the throne in gladness!

"God alone, Creator, fill us with the joy of your presence."

JULY 13

HYMN

"O serve the Lord with gladness," To Him the sovereign ruler,

And glad hosannas bring, The universal King;

SCRIPTURE

Jesus was in the center of the procession, and the people all around him were shouting, "Praise God for the Son of David! Blessings on the one who comes in the name of the Lord! Praise God in highest heaven!" (Matthew 21:9).

MEDITATION

There are different types of exclamations. One is the expletive, that we usually associate with curse words. Some folks cannot contain their anger or surprise, so a curse jumps out of their mouth.

But the same thing can happen with praise. We experience God in such a way that praise words leap from our throats. "Hallelujah!" or "Hosanna!"

Hosanna means "save us!" When the crowd saw King Jesus riding into Jerusalem, they could not be silent but shouted "Hosanna." When we see the sovereign universal Ruler at work in our lives, we cannot help but do the same.

"Hosanna! Lord, save us!"

HYMN

Forever through the ages
His truth unchanging stands;
Let all the nations fear Him,
And reverence His commands.

SCRIPTURE

Praise the Lord, all you nations. Praise him, all you people of the earth (Psalm 117:1).

MEDITATION

Are we a Christian nation? We often debate whether that is true and whether it is a good thing.

What do we mean by that? Do we mean that everyone in the country is a Christian? No. Do we mean the majority are Christian? Do we mean our country was founded on or currently operates on Christian principles?

Or do we mean, "Our country is superior to others because we are on the Lord's side and he is on our side?" We want God to be with our nation, but that quickly becomes a point of pride and superiority.

We must remember that God is the ruler of every nation, whether many or few in a particular nation recognize his rule. All nations and all people are to fear the Lord.

"Lord, bless our nation and every nation. May we follow your rule."

JULY 15

HYMN

"O serve the Lord with gladness," Exalt Him in the highest;

His love to all proclaim; And spread abroad His fame;

SCRIPTURE

I will exalt you, my God and King, and praise your name forever and ever (Psalm 145:1).

MEDITATION

How do we exalt God?

We say and sing words of praise to him. We confess him as the only God, our Lord, the ruler of the universe.

But we must do much more than acknowledge him with our words. If we would truly exalt God, we pay tribute to him with our every action. Obedience is exaltation. We praise not just on Sunday but every hour of every day.

And we exalt him publicly. That does not mean we break out in "Hallelujah" at work or at the store. It means our acts of compassion and duty are open for others to view. We proclaim God's love to all, so they also may exalt him.

"Sovereign Lord, may we lead others to see your fame this day."

JULY 16

HYMN

All majesty, dominion,
All power and glory be
To Him who reigns in triumph,
Through all eternity.

SCRIPTURE

All glory to him who alone is God, our Savior through Jesus Christ our Lord. All glory, majesty, power, and authority are his before all time, and in the present, and beyond all time! Amen (Jude 1:25).

MEDITATION

I only use the word "majesty" in church. On British television, they call the king, "Your majesty." In America, we got rid of our king long ago. We don't like the idea of anyone being above the ordinary people.

I do sometimes use the word "majestic" to try to describe a sublime view.

God, in his glory and power, is majestic. What is more, he is majesty itself. When we ascribe glory, power, authority, and majesty to him, we are not flattering the Lord. We are simply recognizing who and what he is. And that is who he has been, is, and ever will be. He triumphs throughout eternity.

"Lord God, open our eyes and hearts to see your majesty."

JULY 17

HYMN

"O serve the Lord with gladness,"
And come before His throne;
He is our great Redeemer,
And He is God alone.

SCRIPTURE

Then they remembered that God was their rock, that God Most High was their redeemer (Psalm 78:35).

MEDITATION

We serve the Lord with gladness because he is the powerful, majestic, and holy God. When we see God, we break forth in joyous praise.

We rejoice in who God is. We also rejoice because of what God has done for us. He redeemed us, buying us back from sin. God alone initiates salvation. When humanity turned against the Lord, he could have abandoned us. He could have demanded that we meet his standards before we could be reconciled to him. Instead, he sent his Son to die for us while we were still sinners.

We cannot stand in the presence of the majestic and holy God. But God gives us standing through Jesus. We come boldly before the throne of the Almighty King.

"God of love, give us confidence so we may stand before your throne."

JULY 18

HYMN

Rescue the perishing, care for the dying,

Snatch them in pity from sin and the grave;

Weep o'er the erring one, lift up the fallen,

Tell them of Jesus the mighty to save.

SCRIPTURE

Rescue those who are unjustly sentenced to die; save them as they stagger to their death (Proverbs 24:11).

MEDITATION

I appreciate hospice workers. Providing physical, emotional, social, and spiritual comfort to those near death is such a blessing. When my wife's parents were in the last stages of dementia, hospice worked with them and with my wife and me to give genuine comfort.

We are all dying, though we hate to admit it. What is worse than physical death is the spiritual sickness of sin that can lead to separation from God, the source of life. All Christians have a mission to care for those in danger of spiritual death. We point them to Jesus, the life, who saves and gives the deepest comfort possible, the comfort of reconciliation with the God who loves them. We are rescue workers, the first responders for those who have fallen and can't get up.

"Lord, give us a heart of pity for and service to those in danger of death."

JULY 19

HYMN

Though they are slighting Him,
Still He is waiting,

Waiting the penitent child to receive;

Plead with them earnestly, plead with them gently;

He will forgive if they only believe.

SCRIPTURE

The Lord isn't really being slow about his promise, as some people think. No, he is being patient for your sake. He does not want anyone to be destroyed, but wants everyone to repent (2 Peter 3:9).

MEDITATION

I do not like to wait.

Yet the Bible often tells us we must wait for the Lord. He will help on his timetable, not ours.

What is more amazing is that the Lord waits for us. He is not the impatient, out-to-get-us God that some imagine. He is the infinitely patient God who waits for us to return to him. He is the Father of the prodigals who watches the road every day in anticipation of our coming home.

So we plead with others. "Come to your senses. Come back to the path that leads to home. Come back to the loving Father who is eager and waiting to receive you with open arms."

"Patient Father, may we and others hear your plea to return."

JULY
20

HYMN

Down in the human heart,
Crushed by the tempter,
Feelings lie buried that grace can restore;

Touched by a loving heart,
wakened by kindness,
Chords that were broken will vibrate once more.

SCRIPTURE

The Lord is close to the brokenhearted; he rescues those whose spirits are crushed (Psalm 34:18).

MEDITATION

Brokenhearted, crushed, despondent, miserable. We all have felt that way. We are so weighed down by life that we are not sure we can feel anything again. We may go through the motions so that others do not see our despair, but inside we are dead.

Then come kind words from someone who cares. At first, we may not be able to hear the words, but slowly they bring our hearts alive once more.

Today someone who is crushed needs an encouraging word from us. We do not have to search for the right words, the magic words that will heal them. Sometimes we speak most clearly when we do not say a thing. We just show up. We stand beside others. We speak with kind actions. And Jesus, the one who had his own heart broken, works through our words and actions to bring hearts back to life.

"Sensitive Jesus, lead us to the brokenhearted today."

JULY
21

HYMN

Rescue the perishing, Duty demands it;

Strength for thy labor the Lord will provide;

Back to the narrow way patiently win them;

Tell the poor wanderer a Savior has died.

SCRIPTURE

In the same way, when you obey me you should say, "We are unworthy servants who have simply done our duty" (Luke 17:10).

MEDITATION

"Duty" is a word that has almost disappeared in our culture. If you say you are helping someone out of a sense of duty, you are criticized for being insincere. Some say you should only help others if your heart is in it.

If that is true, then few will be helped. Caregiving always becomes routine and a burden. Yes, we assist others out of love, but it is a disciplined love that helps when it is costly and inconvenient. The word for that kind of love is "duty."

So duty demands that we patiently look after those who are lost. When that task becomes tiresome, and it will, we rely on the strength provided by the Lord through the Holy Spirit to enable us to love not with emotion only, but with action.

"Savior, when we are tired of doing good to others, give us strength to love."

HYMN

God of our strength, enthroned above,

The source of life, the fount of love;

O let devotion's sacred flame

Our souls awake to praise Thy name.

SCRIPTURE

Protect me, for I am devoted to you. Save me, for I serve you and trust you. You are my God (Psalm 86:2).

MEDITATION

My friend George is a devoted fisherman. He spends time and money on rod, reel, bait, waders, nets, and other equipment. He gets up before dawn, drives several miles, and stands in a freezing cold river. He continues to fish when he catches nothing. When he does make a catch, there's the gutting and the cleaning and the cooking before the eating.

I never enjoyed fishing. I do not understand those who do. It looks like annoying work to me.

But I do understand that fishing brings joy to my friend George.

Devotion to God requires time, money, discomfort, and patience. But it brings deep joy.

"God of strength and love, inflame our hearts in devoted praise to you."

JULY 23

HYMN

To Thee we lift our joyful eyes,

To Thee on wings of faith we rise;

Come Thou, and let Thy courts on earth

Ring out Thy praise in holy mirth.

SCRIPTURE

A single day in your courts is better than a thousand anywhere else! I would rather be a gatekeeper in the house of my God than live the good life in the homes of the wicked (Psalm 84:10).

MEDITATION

"Courts" here is not a legal term but a royal one. Every king has a court, a group of those who regularly attend him. The temple in Jerusalem had several courtyards where those who sought the presence of the Lord could gather. Israel regularly gathered there on feast days like Passover and Pentecost. These sacred assemblies were times of joy, "holy mirth," when God's people met to praise him.

Today the courts of the Lord are anywhere God's people assemble to worship him. "Going to church" should not be a burden but a time of laughter and delight. Yes, we worship with solemn reverence, but we take pleasure in the presence of the Lord.

"Lord, lift us up on wings of faith into your joyous life."

JULY 24

HYMN

God of our strength, from day to day
Direct our thoughts and guide our way;

O may our hearts united be
In sweet communion, Lord, with Thee.

SCRIPTURE

We know how much God loves us, and we have put our trust in his love. God is love, and all who live in love live in God, and God lives in them (1 John 4:16).

MEDITATION

The Lord is God, and we are not god. There is an infinite qualitative difference between us and God.

The Bible makes this clear in many ways. It says one cannot see God and live. When humans do catch a glimpse of God, they fall face down in humility and awe.

That's why it is so amazing that we humans have communion with God. The relationship we have with the Lord is so personal, so intimate, that we can say that God lives in us, and we live in him. Just as Jesus was in the Father and the Father in him, so through Jesus and the Spirit we have sweet communion with the God beyond our imagination. So we ask God to make us aware of his presence, to direct our thoughts to Him.

"Lord God, give us strength to unite our hearts to you this day."

HYMN

God of our strength, on Thee we call;

God of our hope, our light, our all,

Thy name we praise, Thy love adore,

Our rock, our shield, forevermore.

SCRIPTURE

Let all that I am wait quietly before God, for my hope is in him (Psalm 62:5).

MEDITATION

Hope is in short supply in our time. That has always been true, but it seems like we live in an especially hopeless age. Perhaps that's because of a 24-hour-a-day news cycle that bombards us with stories of disaster, oppression, and injustice.

Hope is different than optimism. Optimism sees signs that things are getting better or could get better with some human effort. Hope faces the bad news head-on but trusts that, despite appearances, the Lord is working to bring healing, safety, and justice to our world.

We must wait for God to act. Our hope is in him alone. But waiting is not a passive acceptance of evil. God is working in his world, and he can work through us. Through prayer, we call on him to work. Through loving service to our neighbors, we show our trust and hope. That service is in the strength and power of God who is at work in all things.

"God of our hope, may we patiently wait and work."

JULY 26

HYMN

Take the world, but give me Jesus,
All its joys are but a name;

But His love abideth ever,
Through eternal years the same.

SCRIPTURE

Do not love this world nor the things it offers you, for when you love the world, you do not have the love of the Father in you (John 2:15).

MEDITATION

"World" means many things in the Bible. God made the world, the created order, and called it good. God so loved the world, that is, all the people in the world. The world is often a good word.

But the Bible also uses "world" to speak of the fallen culture that surrounds us. That world goes its way in rebellion against the Lord. To be worldly is to go along with what most people do and say. Thus, the warning, "Do not love the world."

That rebellious world promises great rewards. We may think we can have it all by following Jesus and also being successful in worldly terms. Jesus says we must choose. We give up that world for the greater and more certain rewards of following our Lord.

"Lord Jesus, this day may we choose to follow genuine joys."

JULY 27

HYMN

Take the world, but give me Jesus,

Sweetest comfort of my soul;

With my Savior watching o'er me,

I can sing though billows roll.

SCRIPTURE

I have told you all this so that you may have peace in me. Here on earth you will have many trials and sorrows. But take heart, because I have overcome the world (John 16:33).

MEDITATION

Choosing Jesus over the world sounds easy. It is not. When we reject what the world sees as valuable, the world strikes back. Those around us ridicule us, saying we are narrow-minded, out-of-touch, and even full of hatred for others. But it is not the people of the world that we reject. God so loved them that he gave his son. We too love them in action, not just in word.

But choosing Jesus over the world invites trials and sorrows. Like Jesus, many misunderstand us, lie about us, and even think they are doing the right thing by opposing us. They put Jesus on the cross. We who follow him should expect the same. Yet he forgave them from the cross and died for them. We also love our enemies, turn the other cheek, and even bless those who persecute. When the world turns against us, we sing in the comfort of his love.

"Lord Jesus, forgive those who harm us. May we show them your love."

JULY 28

HYMN

Take the world, but give me Jesus,

Let me view His constant smile;

Then throughout my pilgrim journey

Light will cheer me all the while.

SCRIPTURE

Jesus spoke to the people once more and said, "I am the light of the world. If you follow me, you won't have to walk in darkness, because you will have the light that leads to life" (John 8:12).

MEDITATION

I have become a morning person, waking up early and eager to see the dawn. As the sun slowly rises, I begin to see the outlines of trees, clouds and flowers. My spirits rise with the sun.

When rain has hidden the light for several days, I long to see the sun and feel its warmth. Light is life-giving.

The smile of Jesus is our light. That is interesting since the gospels never speak of Jesus as smiling. Yet when you read what he said, especially his jokes about swallowing camels or sending the camel through a needle's eye, you must believe he smiled. Smiling or not, Jesus is the light of the world. He lifts our spirits. He cheers our day.

"Light of the world, shine on us today."

JULY 29

HYMN

Take the world, but give me Jesus.

In His cross my trust shall be,

Till, with clearer, brighter vision,

Face to face my Lord I see.

SCRIPTURE

For God, who said, "Let there be light in the darkness," has made this light shine in our hearts so we could know the glory of God that is seen in the face of Jesus Christ (2 Corinthians 4:6).

MEDITATION

Being able to see family and friends virtually through online meetings has been a great blessing. It is a great improvement over a mere telephone conversation. Yet nothing takes the place of seeing them face-to-face.

Many scriptures in the Bible say one cannot see God face to face. Yet some are allowed to view the glory of the Lord. That glory, that essence of God became flesh in Jesus. But we did not see Jesus in the flesh. Yet by faith we do see him as clearly as those disciples who walked with him, even those who saw him in glory on the mountain of transfiguration.

And the day will come when we see him face to face in our resurrected bodies. May each day bring us clearer vision of Jesus until that great day comes.

"Lord Jesus, open our eyes to see the glory of God in you today."

JULY 30

HYMN

Oh, the height and depth of mercy!

Oh, the length and breadth of love!

Oh, the fullness of redemption,

Pledge of endless life above!

SCRIPTURE

And may you have the power to understand, as all God's people should, how wide, how long, how high, and how deep his love is (Ephesians 3:18).

MEDITATION

I have spent my life teaching and preaching about God.

I do not know what I am talking about. By that I mean that God is beyond me. I cannot fully understand him. I cannot describe him. Even those smarter and more spiritual than I am (and there are many) cannot fathom the Almighty.

But this we know. God loves us. Even here, his love is beyond our comprehension. His grace is boundless. Our redemption is complete. The most profound theology I know I learned as a child. "Jesus loves me, this I know for the Bible tells me so."

And when we stand before our Creator at the end, all we need to know is love.

"God of love, open our hearts, minds, and lives to your love."

JULY 31

HYMN

They tell me of a land so fair, Where spring in fadeless beauty blooms,

Unseen by mortal eyes, Beneath unclouded skies.

SCRIPTURE

On each side of the river grew a tree of life, bearing twelve crops of fruit, with a fresh crop each month. The leaves were used for medicine to heal the nations (Revelation 22:2).

MEDITATION

"Unseen by mortal eyes." It's an interesting phrase for a blind hymn writer to use. No doubt Fanny Crosby wanted to see the beauty of Spring beneath a cloudless sky. But what she most wanted to see cannot be seen by mortal eyes.

These words remind us that the beauty we see in our world is just a foretaste of what we will see in the new heavens and earth. Others sometimes accuse Christians of being unrealistic, believing in "pie in the sky when you die by and by." But, by faith we see what is more real, more permanent than what we now see with our eyes. It is the world that God intends. And so we pray to our Father, "Your will be done on earth as it is in heaven," trusting that, even though we cannot see that happening now, that fair land is on the way.

"Father, give us eyes of trust to see the world to come."

AUGUST 1

HYMN

They tell me of a land so fair,
Where all is light and song,
Where angel choirs their anthems join
With yonder blood-washed throng.

SCRIPTURE

And all the angels were standing around the throne and around the elders and the four living beings. And they fell before the throne with their faces to the ground and worshiped God (Revelation 7:11).

MEDITATION

When I was a kid, heaven sounded boring. All we would do forever was to sing praise to God. Even though I like to sing, it does seem like we would get tired of it after a while.

But the new heaven and earth that God promises is beyond time. We cannot imagine an eternal now. So we think of eternity as forever. However, we are never bored in the current moment. We are bored when we look back in time at how long we have been doing the same old thing. Or we are bored, anticipating a future when nothing changes.

The praise we give to God in the new heaven and earth is forever new. We join other created beings, the angels, in constantly expressing our love to the Source of love.

"Father, may we anticipate our constant praise to you."

AUGUST 2

HYMN

No radiant beams from sun or moon
Adorn that land so fair,
For He who sits upon the throne
Shines forth resplendent there.

SCRIPTURE

And the city has no need of sun or moon, for the glory of God illuminates the city, and the Lamb is its light (Revelation 21:23).

MEDITATION

Again, one who is blind longs for light. Creation begins with "Let there be light." That light from God exists even before he makes the sun and moon to give light.

God is light. What does that mean? He is the source of all life. There can be no life without light. He is the light that allows us to see the beauty around us. He enlightens us by showing us the path to happiness.

God's light is often called "glory." We still use that word to describe a "glorious day." One day we will see him in his glory. What's more, that glory will be the only light we need. Fanny Crosby was not the only one who is blind. We blind ourselves to the life, beauty, and guidance from God.

"Glorious God, may we seek your light. Shine on us today."

AUGUST 3

HYMN

O land of light and love and joy, What will our song of triumph be
Where comes no night of care, When we shall enter there!

SCRIPTURE

Its gates will never be closed at the end of day because there is no night there. And all the nations will bring their glory and honor into the city (Revelation 21:25-26).

MEDITATION

Like most kids, I was afraid of the dark. "Leave a light on," I would say when my mother left my room at bedtime.

I no longer leave a light on when I sleep, but I do find myself at times afraid of a deeper darkness. The world seems very dark at times with wars, riots, disease, oppression, crime, and unnumbered threats.

Then there is the darkness of death. Night falls for us all.

The good news is that God has left a light on. He shines in Jesus. And although death seems dark, the threats of the night will be gone in the city of God. No night there.

"Gentle Father, show us your light in the darkness."

AUGUST 4

HYMN

"Eye hath not seen, ear hath not heard,

Neither hath it entered into the heart of man,

The things which God hath prepared for them,

Prepared for them that love Him."

SCRIPTURE

That is what the Scriptures mean when they say, "No eye has seen, no ear has heard, and no mind has imagined what God has prepared for those who love him" (1 Corinthians 2:9).

MEDITATION

I believe Jesus was raised from the dead. What I have trouble believing is that I will be raised from the dead. Death appears so final.

Yet my trouble is not primarily a lack of faith but a failure of imagination. What will it be like after death? What will the Second Coming of Jesus look like? How will it be in the new heaven and earth?

The Bible is not clear on this. It uses metaphors like rest and pearly gates and streets of gold, none of which appeal to me. They seem irrelevant or gaudy. But the Bible uses these descriptions of what is valuable on earth to describe what cannot be described in words. What God has planned for us is better than anything we can imagine.

"Lord God, we love you. Help us imagine the world of love that awaits us."

AUGUST 5

HYMN

Jesus is tenderly calling you home

Calling today, calling today,

Why from the sunshine of love will you roam,

Farther and farther away?

SCRIPTURE

But now, O Jacob, listen to the Lord who created you. O Israel, the one who formed you says, "Do not be afraid, for I have ransomed you. I have called you by name; you are mine" (Isaiah 43:1).

MEDITATION

Home. What a warm and comforting word.

The poet Robert Frost said, "Home is the place where, when you have to go there, they have to take you in."

There are many places where we do not feel at home. We are strangers, exiles, and refugees in our own land. We do not live like the world and the world feels strange to us.

But there is a place where we can rest in comfort, a place where everyone knows our name. Jesus himself calls us by name, claims us as his own, and welcomes us into our true home with him. He tenderly says, "Come home."

"Brother Jesus, may we live at home with you this day."

AUGUST 6

HYMN

Jesus is calling the weary to rest,

Calling today, calling today,

Bring Him your burden and you shall be blest;

He will not turn you away.

SCRIPTURE

Then Jesus said, "Come to me, all of you who are weary and carry heavy burdens, and I will give you rest" (Matthew 11:28).

MEDITATION

The people I am around seem awfully tired. Old people, young people, men, and women live frazzled, overworked lives with no end in sight. When advised to get some rest, they do not see how they can stop or even slow down their pace of living.

Jesus promises rest. He offers a rest that is more than slowing down or stopping. His rest transforms our lives so that even our work becomes a joy not a burden.

To enter that rest we must accept his invitation. To do that requires surrender and practice. We begin by practicing the gift of rest that God offers to his people, the Sabbath he made for them. By letting God take control of one day a week we experience the rest that Jesus promises for every day.

"Jesus, carry our burdens this day. Let us rest in you."

AUGUST 7

HYMN

Jesus is waiting, O come to Him now,

Waiting today, waiting today,

Come with your sins, at His feet lowly bow;

Come, and no longer delay.

SCRIPTURE

There is more than enough room in my Father's home. If this were not so would I have told you that I am going to prepare a place for you? When everything is ready, I will come and get you, so that you will always be with me where I am (John 14:2-3).

MEDITATION

We are used to waiting on people, particularly at doctor's offices. The assumption is that the doctor's time is much more important than our own. If we are late for an appointment, we get canceled and sometimes pay a fee. If the doctor is late, we wait.

So it is stunning to think that Jesus waits for us. Yes, we also wait for the Lord, but he patiently waits for us to hear his voice and respond to his invitation. He prepares a place for us and waits for us to join him.

Let us not selfishly keep him waiting. Let us quickly accept his welcome. Let us bow at his feet and know his forgiveness.

"Welcoming Jesus, move our feet to bow before you as you wait for us."

AUGUST 8

HYMN

Jesus is pleading, O list to His voice,

Hear Him today, hear Him today,

They who believe on His name shall rejoice;

Quickly arise and away.

SCRIPTURE

"Look! I stand at the door and knock. If you hear my voice and open the door, I will come in, and we will share a meal together as friends" (Revelation 3:20).

MEDITATION

I am an introvert, so when someone knocks on my door my first reaction is "Go away."

However, if I am expecting a friend to call or a package delivered, I answer the door quickly.

Jesus is knocking at the door. He is pleading for us to open. What keeps us from rushing to open the door? Perhaps we are afraid of what Jesus will want from us. Perhaps we are too distracted by our own concerns that we fail to hear him knock. Perhaps we think our life, our house, belongs to us and we want no intruders.

But Jesus arrives with the best delivery we can expect. He brings life. He brings himself. He delivers the bread of life and asks us to eat with him.

"Jesus, open the ears of our hearts to hear you knocking."

AUGUST 9

HYMN

Like a wayward child I wandered
From my Father's house away,
But I hear His voice entreating,
And I'm coming home today.

SCRIPTURE

A few days later this younger son packed all his belongings and moved to a distant land, and there he wasted all his money in wild living (Luke 15:13).

MEDITATION

In Luke 15, Jesus tells stories of a lost sheep, a lost coin, and a lost boy. We don't blame the sheep for being lost. It's what sheep do. We don't blame the coin, an inanimate object, for being lost.

We do blame the boy. Rightly so. He is an ingrate who cannot wait for his father to die before receiving his share of the inheritance. He is selfish, pursuing his own pleasures without thinking of the needs of anyone else. He is prodigal, that is wasteful, since he spends his money quickly and has nothing.

Ungrateful, selfish, and foolish. We are that boy. In the same way, we have at times turned our back on the Father's house. The first step in returning is to admit that.

"Loving Father, may we admit our wandering so we might return to you."

AUGUST
10

HYMN

I have wandered in the darkness, But my Father did not leave me,

And my path was lone and drear, He was watching ever near.

SCRIPTURE

So he returned home to his father. And while he was still a long way off, his father saw him coming. Filled with love and compassion, he ran to his son, embraced him, and kissed him (Luke 15:20).

MEDITATION

The ungrateful, selfish, and foolish boy leaves his father and ends up miserable with nothing. Out of love, the father lets him go. He knows what will likely happen to the boy, but he loves him enough to let him find out for himself.

But the father does not abandon his son. He waits and watches for his return.

When we abandon our loving Father, the great and good news is that he never abandons us. He is always watching and waiting for our return. He runs to greet us and receive us back into his embrace.

All he asks is that we turn our feet toward home.

"Father, may we come to our senses and accept your open arms."

AUGUST 11

HYMN

I will ask Him to forgive me
For the wrong that I have done,
To receive, accept and bless me,
Through His well beloved Son.

SCRIPTURE

His son said to him, "Father, I have sinned against both heaven and you, and I am no longer worthy of being called your son" (Luke 15:21).

MEDITATION

The first step toward returning home is admitting we were wrong to leave. The lost boy is hopeful that he can return as a slave, having forfeited his status as a son.

But the father will not hear of it. Before the boy can make his proposal to be merely a servant, the father calls for a robe and a ring and a party.

That is what God has in store for us. Even though we know he will forgive, it is hard for us to admit our sins. Instead, we make excuses, put the blame on others, or speak of those who have done worse than we have. All God asks is that we own our sin. If we do, then by his grace and through His Son, he owns our sin. He accepts us back with robe and ring and party. Let us admit our sin and quit defending our little selves.

"Forgiving Father, kill the pride that keeps us from turning to you."

AUGUST 12

HYMN

O the rapture that awaits me
When I reach my Father's door!
Once within its blest enclosure,
I am safe forevermore.

SCRIPTURE

"And kill the calf we have been fattening. We must celebrate with a feast, for this son of mine was dead and has now returned to life. He was lost, but now he is found." So the party began. (Luke 15:23-24).

MEDITATION

The story of the lost boy is not primarily about the boy who left home and went into the far country. By the end of the story that boy, like the sheep and the coin, is found. He has come home to the place where he is safe evermore.

But there is still a lost boy. While the father completely accepts the prodigal son with great rejoicing, there is one who will not join the party. The older brother had never left home. He was the faithful son who slaved for his father. But now he will not rejoice over the brother who was lost and found. The older brother never left home but he did not understand the father.

If we understand our Father's house, then we rejoice that the door is open to all.

"God, give us your loving heart so we may accept the lost, now found."

AUGUST 13

HYMN

A wonderful Savior is Jesus my Lord,

a wonderful Savior to me.

He hideth my soul in the cleft of the rock,

where rivers of pleasure I see.

SCRIPTURE

As my glorious presence passes by, I will hide you in the crevice of the rock and cover you with my hand until I have passed by (Exodus 33:22).

MEDITATION

After Israel sinned by worshipping the golden calf (Exodus 32), the Lord says he will not go with them to the promised land. Moses intercedes on behalf of God's people and the Lord relents and agrees to go with them. Moses seeks assurance of this, so he asks to see the glorious presence of the Lord. God says that no one can see his face, but he will show his glory to Moses. The Lord hides Moses in the cleft of the rock and protects him with his hand while his glory passes by.

Fanny Crosby connects those two ideas, the gentle protection of God and seeing the glory of the Lord, with Jesus. As our wonderful Savior he reveals the glory of God, and he protects us from all evil with his powerful hand

"Wonderful Jesus, show us the glory of the Lord. Protect us this day."

AUGUST
14

HYMN

A wonderful Savior is Jesus my Lord;

he taketh my burden away.

He holdeth me up, and I shall not be moved;

he giveth me strength as my day.

SCRIPTURE

He gives power to the weak and strength to the powerless (Isaiah 40:29).

MEDITATION

"Give us this day our daily bread."

This is the phrase we pray in the Lord's Prayer. It is more than a plea for daily food (although it is that). We implore our Father to give us everything we need for today. Too often we worry about having enough for the future. We pile up stuff. We save money. We don't know how much we will need to care for us all our lives. All we know is that we never have enough. We want more.

The Lord does not promise enough for a lifetime. He promises strength for today. He asks us to live one day at a time and to give that day to him. In return for that trust, he takes away our daily burden, establishes us for this day, and insures that nothing will shake us today. That's one reason why spending a few moments in meditation on God's word each day grounds us.

"Jesus, give us what we need this day. May we trust each day to you."

AUGUST 15

HYMN

With numberless blessings each moment he crowns, and filled with his fullness divine, I sing in my rapture, "Oh, glory to God for such a Redeemer as mine!"

SCRIPTURE

By his divine power, God has given us everything we need for living a godly life. We have received all of this by coming to know him, the one who called us to himself by means of his marvelous glory and excellence (2 Peter 1:3).

MEDITATION

Teresa of Avila once wrote, "Jesus does not demand great actions from us, but simply surrender and gratitude."

If we surrender ourselves to Jesus daily, he fills us with the fullness of the Divine nature. Father, Son, and Spirit make their home in us. This happens as a free gift. Our great deeds for God do not create the divine within us. It happens through the small, daily actions that show our love for God and neighbor.

At the heart of those small daily acts is gratitude. Jesus gives numberless blessings. We express our thankfulness in rapturous song— "O Glory to God."

"Redeemer, accept our songs, our words, and our acts of gratitude this day."

AUGUST 16

HYMN

When clothed in his brightness, transported

I rise to meet him in clouds of the sky,

his perfect salvation, his wonderful love,

I'll shout with the millions on high.

SCRIPTURE

Then, together with them, we who are still alive and remain on the earth will be caught up in the clouds to meet the Lord in the air. Then we will be with the Lord forever (1 Thessalonians 4:17).

MEDITATION

"Rapture" has become associated with a particular view of the Second Coming of Jesus.

The truth is that the Bible is not completely clear on all the details of Christ's return. How can it be when it is trying to describe a mystery? We have many questions about that Coming, just as those in Thessalonica had in Paul's day.

No doubt Paul did not answer all their questions (or all of ours), but he makes one thing clear. All those who trust Jesus, whether dead or living at his return, will be with the Lord forever.

This calls for rapturous shouting!

"Lord Jesus, come quickly so we may be with you forever."

AUGUST
17

HYMN

He hideth my soul in the cleft of the rock

that shadows a dry, thirsty land.

He hideth my life in the depths of his love,

and covers me there with his hand.

SCRIPTURE

Yes, I will make rivers in the dry wasteland so my chosen people can be refreshed (Isaiah 43:20).

MEDITATION

God covers Moses with his hand in the cleft of the rock. God also takes care of his people by providing water in the desert. He makes the water come from rocks.

I lived for a time in a dry climate. After a while the heat sapped not only my physical energy but it led to a dryness of soul. In the desert one longs for water. In the desert of our culture, we often thirst for truth, for beauty, and for meaning.

The Lord provides all that through his powerful hand. The world does not understand us. Out of that misunderstanding comes hatred for the people of God. We share the good news of the love of Jesus. They respond with ridicule. So it was with Jesus on the cross. But God hid the life of Jesus in his love. He raised him from the dead and vindicated him. In the same way, he hides and covers us with his shielding hand.

"Lord, hide us in your love."

AUGUST
18

HYMN

Be silent, be silent,
A whisper is heard,

Be silent, and listen,
O treasure each word!

SCRIPTURE

For God speaks again and again, though people do not recognize it (Job 33:14).

MEDITATION

I sometimes find it hard to hear in restaurants. Everyone is talking, the music is playing loudly, and there seems to be an echo. I strain forward to try to engage my meal companion in conversation.

Noise also gets in the way of hearing God. That noise is sometimes outside of us. We are too busy trying to hear what others are saying, perhaps too concerned with their approval, that we cannot hear the word of the Lord. More often, the noise is inside. Our monkey-minds chatter away and distract us from listening to God.

God wants to speak to us. We must block out the noise and listen. It takes discipline, that is, consistent practice to be silent and hear his voice. That's why a time set to daily meditate on God's word is so essential.

"Loving God, may we be silent to hear your gentle whisper today."

AUGUST 19

HYMN

Be silent, be silent,   This altar that echoes

For holy this place,   The message of grace.

SCRIPTURE

But the Lord is in his holy Temple. Let all the earth be silent before him. (Habakkuk 2:20).

MEDITATION

In Habakkuk 2:18-19, the prophet makes fun of those who worship idols. He urges those worshippers to shout loudly to their "gods" in order to wake them up. Why must you make a lot of noise to worship an idol? Because the idol cannot hear! That god does not exist!

By contrast, the Lord waits in his holy temple for his people to come to him. We do not need to wake him up or convince him to hear us. We approach him in reverent silence.

There is certainly a place for exuberant praise to the Lord. We sing loudly in our rapture for what he has done for us. But let us not equate "loud" with genuine worship. When we meet together, it is not a rock concert but an entry into the presence of the Almighty God. That God wants to speak to us. Even in exuberant praise, we approach with humble silence to listen. We stand on holy ground.

"Lord of all Creation, we come to you in silent gratitude."

AUGUST 20

HYMN

Be silent, be silent,

Breathe humbly our prayer,

A foretaste of Eden

This moment we share.

SCRIPTURE

But when you pray, go away by yourself, shut the door behind you, and pray to your Father in private. Then your Father, who sees everything, will reward you (Matthew 6:6).

MEDITATION

In the Garden of Eden, God walked and talked with Adam and Eve. They had an intimate relationship with the Almighty, a comfortable companionship.

That was broken when sin entered the world. But now, through Christ, that cherished relationship has been restored. It will be fully restored in the new heaven and earth, when again humanity will see God face to face.

But even now we have a foretaste of that restored Eden. We can enter into the very Presence of the Lord through prayer. We pray to a loving Father who wants to spend time with his children. We enter that secret, private place where we can pour out our hearts to him. We talk to him in a comfortable companionship. He hears us. We listen to him.

"God of love, thanks for the gift of companionship called prayer."

AUGUST
21

HYMN

Be silent, be silent,

His mercy record,

Be silent, be silent

And wait on the Lord.

SCRIPTURE

So the Lord must wait for you to come to him so he can show you his love and compassion. For the Lord is a faithful God. Blessed are those who wait for his help (Isaiah 30:18).

MEDITATION

The Lord longs to show us his love and compassion. He waits on us to return to him.

Why do we keep the Lord waiting?

Because we want to do things our way. We want to come to the Lord when it is convenient for us. We want to be his people as long as we don't go overboard on this "religious stuff." We want to call him "Lord" and then run our own lives.

Still, he waits for us. Faithfully. Patiently.

When we fully (or at least, more fully) turn to the Lord, we find that while he waits for us, now we must wait for him. If he is truly our Lord, he sets the timetable.

"Faithful Lord, as you have waited on us, may we wait on you."

AUGUST 22

HYMN

Tread softly, tread softly,   Tread softly, tread softly,

The Master is here,   He bids us draw near.

SCRIPTURE

But now you have been united with Christ Jesus. Once you were far away from God, but now you have been brought near to him through the blood of Christ (Ephesians 2:13).

MEDITATION

What does it mean to be near to God?

Is it a feeling? We have all felt near to God. Yet that feeling will not last. There are times we feel far away from the Lord.

If you drive to a large city, you often see it long before you arrive. Many times after catching a glimpse of the skyline, the city disappears due to the twists in the road. It looks as if you are farther away, when in fact you are drawing nearer.

So too with God. We cannot trust our feelings when it comes to nearness to God. We cannot even trust our sight. What we must trust is his grace that brings us closer to him through the blood of Christ.

"Father, increase our trust that you have brought us near to you."

AUGUST 23

HYMN

To God be the glory, great things He has done;

So loved He the world that He gave us His Son,

Who yielded His life an atonement for sin,

And opened the life gate that all may go in.

SCRIPTURE

Yes, I am the gate. Those who come in through me will be saved. They will come and go freely and will find good pastures (John 10:9).

MEDITATION

The Bible describes how Jesus saves us—the atonement—in many ways. This hymn says Jesus opened the life gate. He pioneered a path to salvation for us to follow.

Jesus says he not only opened the gate, but that he is the gate. He provides a safe place for his sheep to live, and he leads them out to good pastures. Providing for his flock cost Jesus a death on a cross. He is the Good Shepherd who laid down his life for the sheep.

So we give glory to God who gave his Son to be the way, the path, the gate that leads us to the Father. All God asks is that we enter the gate. Following that path means we also must take up our cross. It means laying down our life for others. It means we give glory to God by our every action. The gate is open. Come in!

"God of love, we give you glory for opening the path for us through Jesus."

AUGUST 24

HYMN

O perfect redemption, the purchase of blood,

To every believer the promise of God;

The vilest offender who truly believes,

That moment from Jesus a pardon receives.

SCRIPTURE

He canceled the record of the charges against us and took it away by nailing it to the cross (Colossians 2:14).

MEDITATION

Another word that describes the atonement is "pardon." We know what it is like for someone to be pardoned for a crime. They admit their fault but receive no punishment. What is more, sometimes the record of the crime is expunged. It's as if the crime never happened.

We may wonder at the justice of pardons. It seems that only the wealthy, influential friends of governors and presidents receive pardons.

When it comes to the pardon we receive from God, it is mercy, not justice that triumphs. But there is no injustice, unfairness, or partiality in God's pardon. Jesus paid the just penalty for our sins on the cross. And pardon is for all who trust in Jesus, even the vilest offender. Even me. Even us.

"Lord God, thank you for removing even the record of the charges against us."

AUGUST 25

HYMN

Great things He has taught us, great things He has done,

And great our rejoicing through Jesus the Son;

But purer, and higher, and greater will be

Our wonder, our transport, when Jesus we see.

SCRIPTURE

Dear friends, we are already God's children, but he has not yet shown us what we will be like when Christ appears. But we do know that we will be like him, for we will see him as he really is (1 John 3:2).

MEDITATION

Many have misunderstood Christian hope. Some think Christians have no concern for justice now. We only need to tough it out until Jesus comes. They say our emphasis on heaven makes us of no use on earth.

The truth is that God has already done great things for all people on earth. He loved so much that he gave his Son that the world might be saved. He has blessed us beyond imagination.

But we believe greater things are still to come. Our wonder will be even greater when we see Jesus face to face.

"Loving Jesus, we long to see you."

AUGUST 26

HYMN

Praise the Lord, praise the Lord,

Let the earth hear his voice!

Praise the Lord, praise the Lord,

Let the people rejoice!

O come to the Father, through Jesus the Son,

And give Him the glory, great things He has done

SCRIPTURE

Sing to the Lord, for he has done wonderful things. Make known his praise around the world (Isaiah 12:5).

MEDITATION

When we think of all that God has done for us, we break out in praise!

That praise is to be proclaimed throughout the earth. We Christians have spent too much time moaning over the evil state of the world. We sometimes think we are helping others by telling them how bad they are.

They know that. People know the brokenness of the world.

Instead, we bring good news. God has done great things! God loves all people! He wants to bless them beyond their imagination. The whole earth should hear his loving voice.

"Great God, may we shout your praise to all we meet this day, by word and deed."

AUGUST 27

HYMN

One blessed hour with Jesus our Lord,

One blessed hour to feast on His Word;

One blessed hour with Jesus apart,

One blessed hour to calm the troubled heart.

SCRIPTURE

Then Jesus said, "Let's go off by ourselves to a quiet place and rest awhile." He said this because there were so many people coming and going that Jesus and his apostles didn't even have time to eat (Mark 6:31).

MEDITATION

We may think Jesus lived in a simpler time when the pace of life was slower. Yet life was hard in his day. People worked hard from morning to night just to eke out a living.

Jesus and his followers were diligent workers. The disciples had just spent time on a ministry tour, teaching all day in a village then going to the next. The terrible news of the death of John the Baptist at the hand of Herod had just reached Jesus.

What did Jesus and the disciples need after hard work and bad news? They needed to be alone with God. When we are tired from overwork and sorrow, we need the same. An hour alone with Jesus.

"Gentle Jesus, draw us into that time of rest and prayer with you."

AUGUST
28

HYMN

One blessed hour with Jesus to plead,

One blessed hour to tell Him our need;

One blessed hour refreshing and sweet,

One blessed hour to sit at Jesus' feet.

SCRIPTURE

As Jesus and the disciples continued on their way to Jerusalem, they came to a certain village where a woman named Martha welcomed him into her home. Her sister, Mary, sat at the Lord's feet, listening to what he taught (Luke 10:38-39).

MEDITATION

We know the story of Mary and Martha. Martha prepares the meal while Mary listens to Jesus. Martha then wants Jesus to tell Mary to help her. Instead, Jesus says that Mary has chosen to do the better thing.

Let's not be too hard on Martha. She is serving Jesus. What she (and perhaps we) fails to see is that working harder is not the only calling we have. There is a time to work for Jesus but there is a time for sitting, resting, and listening. There is a time to make our pleas to Jesus. A time to rely on his strength and wisdom instead of on our own. Like Martha, we are overly concerned with getting things done. Jesus says, "Come sit for a while."

"Jesus, make us sit and listen."

AUGUST
29

HYMN

One blessed hour from labor to rest,

One blessed hour to lean on His breast;

Loving and loved, His favor to share,

One blessed hour of soul reviving prayer.

SCRIPTURE

But Jesus often withdrew to the wilderness for prayer (Luke 5:15).

MEDITATION

Jesus, the eternal Son of God felt the need to pray. He did not rely upon his own strength, but on the power of his Father. When Jesus faced hurting, needy people he went to his Father for power to heal them. When threatened by his opponents, Jesus leaned upon the Lord of hosts to protect him. When Jesus wondered where to go and what to do next, he spent time with his Father and received guidance. When exhausted from teaching and healing, Jesus received rest in his time alone with God.

If Jesus, the eternal Son of God, needed to make time to be alone with God, how much more do we need to schedule time alone with the One who loves us. We enter the presence of the Almighty God with Jesus at our side. We enter through the power of the Spirit. Spending time with Father, Son, and Spirit revives our souls. It gives us strength to love.

"Holy Trinity, thank you for the gift of being with you in prayer."

AUGUST
30

HYMN

One blessed hour with Jesus our King,

One blessed hour to speak and to sing;

One blessed hour with Jesus, how dear!

Surely 'tis Heav'n, and Heav'n itself is here.

SCRIPTURE

I long to go and be with Christ, which would be far better for me (Philippians 1:23).

MEDITATION

I've known Christians who talk often of going to heaven. They think of beautiful mansions, streets of gold, and pearly gates.

Do you think you will enjoy heaven? It may seem like a silly question. Of course we will! We especially prefer it to the alternative place.

But the essence of heaven is being with God—Father, Son, and Spirit.

Do we enjoy being with God now? Do we long for the time each day that we have set aside to be aware of his presence, to come to him boldly in prayer? Or do we avoid a quiet time with God? Are we too busy? Does even the idea seem dry and boring?

If we do not enjoy being with God now, what makes us think we will enjoy it eternally?

"Jesus, let us enjoy time with you today."

AUGUST 31

HYMN

One sweet hour of holy, calm delight,
One sweet hour of tender, melting love;
One sweet hour, O precious Savior,
One sweet hour with Thee.

SCRIPTURE

Don't worry about anything; instead, pray about everything. Tell God what you need, and thank him for all he has done. Then you will experience God's peace, which exceeds anything we can understand. His peace will guard your hearts and minds as you live in Christ Jesus (Philippians 4:6-7).

MEDITATION

Daily tasks wear us out. I have to shave every day. We wash clothes only to wash them again. The daily commute, the constant errands, and the changeless chores bring fatigue.

It can be the same with our relationship to God. We pray the same old prayers, fight the same old temptations, and live with the same troublesome people. One challenge to our faith is that today looks much like yesterday and tomorrow will look much like today. If we have a time of prayer each day, it may look like one more tiresome task. But if we make our requests to God, we find that is one daily act that brings peace beyond understanding.

"Jesus, may our daily time with you bring us peace."

SEPTEMBER 1

HYMN

Sing on, ye joyful pilgrims, My faith is heav'nward rising

Nor think the moments long; With every tuneful song;

SCRIPTURE

I walked among the crowds of worshipers, leading a great procession to the house of God, singing for joy and giving thanks amid the sound of a great celebration! (Psalm 42:4).

MEDITATION

The Bible often describes God's people as pilgrims, strangers, foreigners, and exiles. Even in our own land we do not fully belong.

Being a pilgrim can be upsetting. Others think we are strange. We do not fit in. They misunderstand us and falsely accuse us of hatred and subversion of the culture.

But this is a joyful pilgrimage. Something inside us knows we are not at home here, but we are going to our true home. We can joyfully sing in the face of misunderstanding and prejudice against us because we know we are at home with God. And we know that each step that we take on our pilgrimage leads us closer to our final home—the new heaven and earth where the Lord is with us face to face.

"Father God, may we be at home with you this day as we joyfully await our final home."

SEPTEMBER 2

HYMN

Lo! on the mount of blessing,
The glorious mount, I stand;
And looking over Jordan,
I see the promised land.

SCRIPTURE

Then the Lord said to Moses, "This is the land I promised on oath to Abraham, Isaac, and Jacob when I said, 'I will give it to your descendants.' I have now allowed you to see it with your own eyes, but you will not enter the land" (Deuteronomy 34:4).

MEDITATION

I remember when I first heard the story of Moses as a child in Sunday School. When we got to the part where God did not allow Moses to enter the Promised Land, I shouted "That's not fair!" Such exclamations were not welcome in Bible class, but the teacher patiently explained that God was fair and just.

Later, Martin Luther King would apply this story of Moses seeing the land but not allowed to enter it to King's own experience. King did not fully experience civil rights in America, but he saw the day when it would happen. We will not see all that God has promised in our lifetimes, but like Moses, we trust it will come.

"Lord, open our eyes in faith to see what you have promised to your people."

SEPTEMBER 3

HYMN

Sing on, ye joyful pilgrims, / Let songs of home and Jesus
While here on earth we stay; / Beguile each fleeting day;

SCRIPTURE

For this world is not our permanent home; we are looking forward to a home yet to come (Hebrews 13:14).

MEDITATION

I love to travel. I've visited forty-seven states and forty-two countries. Yet, no matter how good the trip, the best part is coming home. The long flights and drives are so much shorter when they lead back to my own house and family.

We Christians long for a home we have not seen. We are nostalgic for a place we have never been. We cannot accurately describe it. Even the Bible must use word pictures for that home—a garden, a house with many rooms, a great city coming down from the sky.

Our picture of that home may be hazy, but our longing for it is real. Each moment we spend alone with God, each beautiful sunrise we witness, each smile of a child, each tear a friend helps wipe away—in all these moments we catch a beguiling glimpse of home.

"Jesus, draw us nearer to our home. Give us a glimpse of it today."

SEPTEMBER

4

HYMN

Sing on the grand old story
Of His redeeming love,
The everlasting chorus
That fills the realms above.

SCRIPTURE

And they sang a new song with these words: "You are worthy to take the scroll and break its seals and open it. For you were slaughtered, and your blood has ransomed people for God from every tribe and language and people and nation" (Revelation 5:9).

MEDITATION

I don't know anyone who does not like some type of music. Even those with a tin ear who cannot carry a tune or play an instrument appreciate some form of music.

When I hear a symphony play a classical composition, my heart says, "Yes! There is beauty in the world. There is a God of beauty." And classical music is not my favorite. Instead, like many people, I have a personal playlist of songs in my head that goes with me through the day, songs mostly from my youth that have stood the test of time.

There is a grander song, a more majestic playlist that awaits us. It is the song of creation, redemption, and glory.

"God of song, may we join angels, saints, and all creation in praising you."

SEPTEMBER
5

HYMN

Sing on, ye joyful pilgrims,
The time will not be long,
Till in our Father's kingdom
We swell a nobler song;

SCRIPTURE

"And you have caused them to become a Kingdom of priests for our God. And they will reign on the earth" (Revelation 5:10).

MEDITATION

"Your kingdom come, your will be done on earth as it is in heaven." This is the prayer Jesus taught his disciples to pray.

What is the kingdom of God?

All creation is his kingdom. God made everything and rules over everything that exists. But it does not look that way. There is a usurper in the kingdom, a false king who claims to hold sway over the earth. He rules by deception. Yet Satan, the great deceiver, has been defeated by the cross and the empty tomb. His days are numbered. The day will come when every knee bows and every tongue confesses that Jesus is Lord. All will worship God as their rightful King.

The time will not be long. And on that day, we will sing.

"Lord Jesus, come quickly so the earth will do the will of God."

SEPTEMBER

HYMN

Where angels there are waiting

To greet us on the shore,

We'll meet beyond the river,

Where surges roll no more.

SCRIPTURE

"We will use these stones to build a memorial. In the future your children will ask you, 'What do these stones mean?' Then you can tell them, 'They remind us that the Jordan River stopped flowing when the Ark of the Lord's Covenant went across.' These stones will stand as a memorial among the people of Israel forever" (Joshua 4:6-7).

MEDITATION

The Bible tells of God's people crossing the Jordan River to enter the promised land. Slaves in the American South used that story to speak of crossing the boundary from South to North in search of freedom, a boundary that sometimes was a literal river, like the Ohio.

"Crossing the Jordan" has also become a metaphor for death. We cross into the land of promise, the land where angels wait to greet us, the land where the waters will no longer threaten us. The land of freedom. Death is frightening, like crossing a raging river. But the God who led his people through the river on dry land will lead us safely through.

"Lord God, lead us safely through death to life."

SEPTEMBER 7

HYMN

Sing on, O blissful music!   My heart is filled with rapture,

With every note you raise,   My soul is lost in praise;

SCRIPTURE

Let the message about Christ, in all its richness, fill your lives. Teach and counsel each other with all the wisdom he gives. Sing psalms and hymns and spiritual songs to God with thankful hearts (Colossians 3:16).

MEDITATION

There are certain feelings that cannot be expressed except through music. This book is a homage to Fanny J. Crosby and to all hymnwriters. Their words of poetry move us deeply. Yet their words would have lost much of their power if there had been no music put to them. Crosby was an accomplished musician, but almost all of the music to her hymns was written by others. As you have read her words, you have heard those tunes and likely sung many of them.

In the assembly of God's people, I have been deeply moved by prayers, sermons, and testimonies I have heard. But my most profound experiences of God have come through song. Truly my heart has been filled with rapture and my soul lost in praise.

"Tuneful God, give us the bliss and ecstasy of your presence in song."

SEPTEMBER

8

HYMN

Dwell in me, O blessed Spirit, In the way of life eternal,

How I need Thy help divine! Keep, oh, keep this heart of mine.

SCRIPTURE

But you are not controlled by your sinful nature. You are controlled by the Spirit if you have the Spirit of God living in you. (And remember that those who do not have the Spirit of Christ living in them do not belong to him at all) (Romans 8:9).

MEDITATION

There is a battle between our sinful nature and our new nature in Christ. A more literal translation for "sinful nature" is "flesh." When the Bible uses this word, it does not refer to literal flesh on the body. God made our bodies and will renew them in the new creation. Sins of the flesh also include more than sexual sins, as if they were worse than others. To Paul, "flesh" is that inward part of us that wants to have our way instead of following God. We can fight that impulse but on our own we lose the struggle and are miserable.

But we are not on our own. The sinful nature does not control us. The Spirit does! The Holy Spirit keeps our hearts and gives us help.

"Holy Spirit, live in us! Control us this day."

SEPTEMBER 9

HYMN

Let me feel Thy sacred presence;
Then my faith will ne'er decline;
Comfort Thou and help me onward,
Fill with love this heart of mine.

SCRIPTURE

And this hope will not lead to disappointment. For we know how dearly God loves us, because he has given us the Holy Spirit to fill our hearts with his love (Romans 5:5).

MEDITATION

Faith, hope, love, and the Holy Spirit connect in this hymn and in this scripture.

God pours his love into our hearts through the Spirit. Heart in the Bible is the seat not only of emotion but of will. With our hearts we experience God's deep love. That love also shapes our will, conforming it to God's.

Feeling the Sacred Presence increases our trust in God. Our faith cannot decline because we are assured that God loves us as his sons and daughters.

And the comfort that outpouring of love gives us also makes us certain of our hope. We know the God that loves us now will continue to lavish his love on all creation.

"Holy Spirit, increase our faith, hope, and love."

SEPTEMBER 10

HYMN

Round the cross where Thou hast led me,

Let my purest feelings twine;

With the blood from sin that cleansed me,

Seal anew this heart of mine.

SCRIPTURE

And he has identified us as his own by placing the Holy Spirit in our hearts as the first installment that guarantees everything he has promised us (1 Corinthians 1:22).

MEDITATION

Literally the scripture above says God has "sealed us with the Holy Spirit in our hearts."

Once letters and important documents were given official seals to ensure their genuineness and importance. We still do this today when we go to a notary for an official seal. God has placed his official seal on our hearts, showing that we belong to him alone. That seal is the Holy Spirit.

The Spirit is also spoken of as a "down payment" of all that God has promised us. We all know that a down payment is just the first of many payments. In the same way, when we think of all that God has done for us, it is just the beginning of what he has yet to give us.

"Holy Spirit, seal our hearts. May we trust you as the down payment for all that is promised."

SEPTEMBER 11

HYMN

Dwell in me, O blessed Spirit,
Gracious teacher, friend divine,
For the home of bliss that waits me
O prepare this heart of mine.

SCRIPTURE

When the Spirit of truth comes, he will guide you into all truth. He will not speak on his own but will tell you what he has heard. He will tell you about the future (John 16:13).

MEDITATION

I have spent my life as a student and a teacher. In my early years as a teacher, I took a "just the facts" approach. I was teaching a subject.

As I learned to teach, I realized I was teaching more than a subject, I was teaching students. The relationship I had with them in class and out was more educational than merely teaching the facts.

Jesus is our teacher. The subject he teaches is himself. We want to do more than know about him, we want to have that knowledge of the one who is the Truth. Jesus shares himself with us through the Holy Spirit. The Spirit guides us into the truth of the one who controls the future.

"Guiding Spirit, teach us to know Jesus, the Truth."

SEPTEMBER
12

HYMN

Dwell in me, oh, dwell in me;

Hear and grant my prayer to Thee;

Spirit, now from Heav'n descending,

Come, oh, come and dwell in me.

SCRIPTURE

But you, dear friends, must build each other up in your most holy faith, pray in the power of the Holy Spirit (Jude 1:20).

MEDITATION

It sounds strange, but in my early years as a Christian I was taught that the Holy Spirit did not dwell in me. I was to follow the Bible and be good on my own power. This led me to hopelessness and despair. I could not be good on my own.

However, since those who taught me this pointed me to the Bible, I began to read more of it. What I found was that the Spirit was on almost every page. I found that the Bible said the Spirit did live in me, assure me, teach me, and comfort me.

That changed how I prayed. I had always prayed to the Father in the name of Jesus. Now I did that through the power of the Holy Spirit. Knowing that the Spirit lives in me changed my whole life. He lives in you, too.

"Holy Spirit, thank you for taking our burden of self-righteousness away."

SEPTEMBER 13

HYMN

He knows: let this my comfort be;

He knows the path designed for me;

A healing balm for all my woes

O blessed thought! my Savior knows.

SCRIPTURE

"I am the good shepherd; I know my own sheep, and they know me" (John 10:14).

MEDITATION

Who knows you?

"Hundreds of people know me," you might say. But who really knows you? Who knows you inside and out, at your best and worst?

If you have a good marriage, it is your husband or wife. They have known you for years, seen every side of you, and still, they love you. Or perhaps it is a friend with whom you can share anything. They know you better than anyone, yet they still remain your friend.

Jesus knows us. He knows us better than wife or husband or friend knows us. He knows us better than we know ourselves. We may hide our true self from others or even from ourselves, but we cannot hide from Jesus. He knows us and still loves us.

"Friend Jesus, may we take comfort in the truth that you know us."

SEPTEMBER 14

HYMN

The thorns that pierce my weary feet;

The low'ring clouds, the storms that beat;

And then, with bliss of calm repose,

O blessed thought! my Savior knows.

SCRIPTURE

This High Priest of ours understands our weaknesses, for he faced all of the same testings we do, yet he did not sin (Hebrews 4:15).

MEDITATION

"I understand."

We've all heard those words from others. I must admit when I hear them, I am a bit skeptical. I want to say (but I don't), "Do you really? How can you understand what I'm going through. Your experience is not mine."

There are even those folks who say, "I understand," only because they want an excuse to share their own troubles.

Jesus understands. God came so close to us that he became one of us. Jesus knows heartache, betrayal, temptation, fatigue, and disappointment. That's why he can help us.

"Suffering Jesus, share our weakness and pain this day."

SEPTEMBER

15

HYMN

He knows: let this suffice for me;
He knows the end I cannot see;
Then let my anxious heart be still,
And patient, wait my Savior's will.

SCRIPTURE

But Lord, be merciful to us, for we have waited for you. Be our strong arm each day and our salvation in times of trouble (Isaiah 33:2).

MEDITATION

There are people I love who are in deep trouble. They struggle with addiction, anger, and violent impulses. They are a danger to themselves and others. I cannot "fix" them and make everything good in their lives. I do what I can. Above all, I pray.

I'd like to know how their lives will turn out. Will they come to their senses? Will they get the help they need to turn their lives around? I've had other loved ones that God set on a better path. Will it happen to these young ones?

What Jesus asks is that we intercede for those we love and then leave it to him. This doesn't mean we abandon our loved ones. It means we trust them to the one who loves them more than we do, the one who knows their future.

"Savior Jesus, save those we love from harm. Bring them into your glorious future."

SEPTEMBER 16

HYMN

My prayer for strength to Him is known,

Tho' breathed in secret and alone;

The weary heart, the tear that flows,

O blessed thought! my Savior knows!

SCRIPTURE

But when you pray, go away by yourself, shut the door behind you, and pray to your Father in private. Then your Father, who sees everything, will reward you (Matthew 6:6).

MEDITATION

Remember privacy? It doesn't seem to exist anymore. Cameras are everywhere, watching every move. You are tracked by advertisers on your phone no matter where you go. Companies and government agencies can find out all about you at the click of a button. And people voluntarily share on social media for all the world to see what should remain private.

Prayer is still between us and God. Yes, Jesus warned of those who liked to be seen to pray. But true prayer is in that secret place between our heart and the heart of a Savior who knows our troubles. The Spirit helps in that prayer by expressing what our words fail to say. And we pray to a gentle, loving Father who quiets our doubts and fears.

Whenever we pray in private, God hears, God knows.

"God, from the depths of our hearts we cry to you, the one who knows us."

SEPTEMBER 17

HYMN

Come, ye who from your hearts believe
That Jesus answers prayer,
Come boldly to a throne of grace
And claim His promise there.

SCRIPTURE

So let us come boldly to the throne of our gracious God. There we will receive his mercy, and we will find grace to help us when we need it most (Hebrews 4:16).

MEDITATION

What is it like to enter the throne room of God?

I think of the tours I have taken of royal places. There, in a huge and ornate room sits a gold-covered throne. When the monarch is present, one enters with respect and a bit of fear. If some countries, one still bows low before the king.

How much more intimidating is it to enter the Presence of God. Yet that is what we do in prayer. We come into the throne room of the Almighty, heads bowed or completely prostrate before him.

But through Christ, we also come boldly. We claim the promises.

"Awesome God, we bow in your Presence. We boldly accept your gifts."

SEPTEMBER
18

HYMN

That, if His love in us abide
And we in Him are one,

Whatever in His name we ask
It surely will be done.

SCRIPTURE

You can ask for anything in my name, and I will do it, so that the Son can bring glory to the Father (John 14:13).

MEDITATION

It's one of the most astounding promises in the Bible. Jesus says he will do anything we ask. No exceptions.

It's also one of the biblical promises that has caused much discussion. Anything? Surely there are selfish prayers that Jesus will not answer. He cannot say yes to prayers that would harm the innocent. In my experience, I'm glad Jesus did not give me everything I asked for in prayer. What I thought I wanted turned out not to be the best for me.

So does Jesus not mean what he says, "Ask for anything?" He certainly does. But we also must ask in his name. This is more than a magic formula. To ask in the name of Jesus means we pray as Jesus prayed, "Not my will but yours be done."

"Jesus, make us bold to ask in your name. May we trust the will of the Father."

SEPTEMBER 19

HYMN

If in the "fountain filled with blood"

Our sins are washed away

Come boldly to a throne of grace,

Rejoicing that we may.

SCRIPTURE

But if we are living in the light, as God is in the light, then we have fellowship with each other, and the blood of Jesus, his Son, cleanses us from all sin (1 John 1:7).

MEDITATION

Some criticize Christianity for being so "bloody." They disapprove of all the talk of blood redemption not just out of squeamishness, but because they think it turns God into a tyrant who demands bloody sacrifices before he will forgive.

This is a misunderstanding of God, of redemption, of sacrifice, and of blood. Blood is life. We hear that on the ads that urge us to donate blood, the gift of life. Sacrifices were not to appease a God who is reluctant to forgive. They were a way of showing the seriousness of the breach between us and God. Redemption is a buying back of someone in slavery. Redemption requires a high price, a life for a life. And God is so eager to forgive us, that he provides the price, the sacrifice, the blood himself. We rejoice as blood-bought people.

"God of love, thank you for the blood of Jesus, the great price of your love."

SEPTEMBER 20

HYMN

Come boldly to a throne of grace,
And bless the Lord our king
Who fills our grateful hearts with praise,
And tunes our tongues to sing.

SCRIPTURE

We were filled with laughter, and we sang for joy. And the other nations said, "What amazing things the Lord has done for them" (Psalm 126:2).

MEDITATION

Children know how to receive gifts. If you give a child a small gift, say a piece of candy, their eyes light up, they flash a grin, then gobble it down with gusto. Yes, their parents may be nearby and tell them to say, "Thank you," but the words are not really necessary. You know the kid is thankful.

By contrast, when adults receive an unexpected gift, they may say, "Thank you," but they are really thinking of why you gave them the gift and how they will pay you back.

We need to receive the unexpected gifts from God with childlike gratitude. We laugh and sing. Our eyes light up and we grin. We may express our gratitude with words, but the focus is on the great Giver, not on our ability to repay or be thankful.

"Giving God, may we delight in your grace, praising you with our every action."

SEPTEMBER 21

HYMN

From every precious, golden hour

We spend in fervent prayer,

We gather strength from day to day

For each returning care.

SCRIPTURE

Pray in the Spirit at all times and on every occasion. Stay alert and be persistent in your prayers for all believers everywhere (Ephesians 6:18).

MEDITATION

If a husband and wife only spoke to each other when they wanted something, would you think that a good marriage?

Yet that is the view that many have of prayer. Some quit praying because they asked God for something and did not get it.

We are encouraged to ask for anything in the name of Jesus. Yet those requests are part of a deeper relationship we have with him. The strength we receive from him is not removal of all difficulties. Instead, spending time with Jesus in prayer draws us closer into his life. We begin to pray as he prayed. We pray in the Spirit. We pray for others. The cares we face may return but now we do not face them alone.

"Jesus, may we come to know you in prayer. Draw us into your life of service."

SEPTEMBER
22

HYMN

And, while with true, believing hearts

We bow before His throne,

There's not a promise He has made

But we may call our own.

SCRIPTURE

And because of his glory and excellence, he has given us great and precious promises. These are the promises that enable you to share his divine nature and escape the world's corruption caused by human desires (2 Peter 1:4).

MEDITATION

"Promises are made to be broken." It's a cliché that we all have experienced as true. The government, bosses, and friends have all broken promises to us. Even those closest to us—husband, wife, children, and parents—have sometimes not kept their promises.

How do you know someone will keep a promise? History and character. If they have kept their word in the past, they are likely to keep it in the future. If they are people of character, you can trust their promises.

How can we trust the promises of God? He has kept his word in the past. He has proven his righteous character. We can own his promises.

"Trustworthy God, increase our trust in your promises."

SEPTEMBER 23

HYMN

Come lovingly and trustingly,   For He has said, "the prayer of faith

Take Jesus at His word,   Was never yet unheard."

SCRIPTURE

"Keep on asking, and you will receive what you ask for. Keep on seeking, and you will find. Keep on knocking, and the door will be opened to you" (Matthew 7:7).

MEDITATION

How do you know when your children really want something? You don't pay attention to all their requests. They want something new every minute! And not everything they desire is good for them.

So you wait until they ask for the same thing over and over. Then you consider whether they can handle what they request. Then you might give it to them.

So also with us and God. Persistence in prayer is not talking God into giving us what we want by wearing him down. Instead, we keep asking, seeking, and knocking because we trust our Father knows what we need better than we know. Our persistence shows the depth of our desire. It also shows what we want most of all—that God's will be done.

"Father, you know what we need. Give us what you desire."

SEPTEMBER 24

HYMN

Safe in the arms of Jesus,
Safe on His gentle breast,
There by His love o'ershaded,
Sweetly my soul shall rest.

SCRIPTURE

"I have told you all this so that you may have peace in me. Here on earth you will have many trials and sorrows. But take heart, because I have overcome the world" (John 16:33).

MEDITATION

We are obsessed with safety. Advertisers bombard us with offers for security services, alarms, locks, and cameras. We spend hundreds of billions of dollars as a country on the armed forces to make us secure. Some are too afraid to leave their own homes. They have seen too many stories of violent crime.

It's impossible for me to even imagine what it must have been like to be a blind woman in New York City in her day, but that is what Fanny Crosby faced. No wonder, by some accounts, this hymn, "Safe in the Arms of Jesus," was her favorite.

What she knew is that nothing in this world—armies, police, or security firms—can insure our safety. Only the arms of Jesus can make us truly safe.

"Gentle Jesus, protect us from all harm today."

SEPTEMBER
25

HYMN

Hark! 'tis the voice of angels,

Borne in a song to me,

Over the fields of glory,

Over the jasper sea.

SCRIPTURE

Therefore, angels are only servants—spirits sent to care for people who will inherit salvation (Hebrews 1:14).

MEDITATION

There are many misunderstandings of angels. Some think we become angels after our death, but the Bible does not say that. Angels are a different order of creation than humans. Some think angels look like chubby babies with wings. But in the Bible, angels look fearsome, so much so that they are always warning us not to be afraid.

Some see no need for angels. If God takes care of us, can he not do so himself without unnecessary intermediaries like angels? Yes, he can. Sometimes he does.

But direct encounters with the Almighty are too overwhelming for most of us. God cares enough to use angels to buffer his awesome presence. Angels are envoys from God to us and for us. In faith we hear their song of protection and safety.

"Father, surround us with your protecting angels."

SEPTEMBER 26

HYMN

Safe in the arms of Jesus,
Safe from corroding care,
Safe from the world's temptations,
Sin cannot harm me there.

SCRIPTURE

The temptations in your life are no different from what others experience. And God is faithful. He will not allow the temptation to be more than you can stand. When you are tempted, he will show you a way out so that you can endure (Hebrews 10:13).

MEDITATION

Most of us have a besetting sin, a sin we have fought all our lives, but we cannot seem to overcome. We might fight the temptation for a day or a week or even longer, but then it returns in full force. We might be tempted to despair that we will ever overcome it.

The key to conquering those sins is not to try harder or fight longer. The key is to rest in the arms of Jesus, to trust that the temptation will not overwhelm us. We rest in the grace that covers all sin. That gives us the power not to give up, to endure.

Resting in Jesus is the key to endurance. We may get knocked down by the sin, but we get up again. Jesus keeps us safe.

"Gentle Jesus, protect us when tempted. May we rest in your grace."

SEPTEMBER 27

HYMN

Free from the blight of sorrow,
Free from my doubts and fears;

Only a few more trials,
Only a few more tears.

SCRIPTURE

For the Lamb on the throne will be their Shepherd. He will lead them to springs of life-giving water. And God will wipe every tear from their eyes (Revelation 7:17).

MEDITATION

When do we cry?

When we are in physical pain. When we have lost those we love. When we are frustrated by doubt. When we are afraid.

Some of us do not cry much. We swallow the pain, the sorrow, the doubt, and the fear. We internalize it and it eats us up from the inside. Tears sometimes can be a good release.

But better still is to have no reason for tears. No pain, sorrow, doubt, nor fear. That is what God promises us through Jesus. In his arms we will be free from all that makes us cry. Even now he assures us that our tears will not last long. Even now he shares our pain, sorrow, doubts, and fears. He cries with us until the day he wipes away all tears.

"Weeping Jesus, share our griefs today."

SEPTEMBER 28

HYMN

Jesus, my heart's dear refuge, Firm on the Rock of Ages,

Jesus has died for me; Ever my trust shall be.

SCRIPTURE

For he will rescue you from every trap and protect you from deadly disease (Psalm 91:3).

MEDITATION

Where do you go to hide? To be safe? To get away from it all?

Perhaps there is a special place you go. Maybe it's not a place but a person you run to. Someone who accepts you and makes you feel safe.

God is often called a refuge for his people. He is a rock, a fortress that protects them. He is the shepherd who looks for them, finds them, and takes them into his arms. He is a loving mother who gathers her young ones under her sheltering arms.

So we put our trust in the Father, in Jesus, in the Spirit who are our refuge. When we need to get away from it all, we know God is always there to accept us and make us feel safe. Since Jesus died for us, how much more is he living to comfort us.

"Jesus, our refuge, may we run to you for safety."

SEPTEMBER 29

HYMN

Here let me wait with patience,
Wait till the night is o'er;
Wait till I see the morning
Break on the golden shore.

SCRIPTURE

I waited patiently for the Lord to help me, and he turned to me and heard my cry (Psalm 40:1).

MEDITATION

I've never had much patience. I want what I want and I want it now. I remember my parents often telling me to be patient. What they did not tell me is how to develop patience.

We develop patience by waiting.

We endure. We put up with pain, uncertainty, and inconvenience. We wait it out.

I remember overhearing a group of older Christian women talking about their aches and pains. After a while the oldest in the group said, "Just live with it!"

That's good advice. Sure, we should do all we can to alleviate pain, sorrow, suffering, and injustice. But there comes a point where we just have to live with it patiently. But we wait in trust that the night will soon be over. Morning will come.

"Patient Jesus, help us to wait in trust."

SEPTEMBER
30

HYMN

Praise our creator and Savior eternal,

Him who redeemed us from death and the grave;

Sing of His greatness, O hail and adore Him,

Strong to deliver, and mighty to save.

SCRIPTURE

Christ is the visible image of the invisible God. He existed before anything was created and is supreme over all creation, for through him God created everything in the heavenly realms and on earth (Colossians 1:15-16).

MEDITATION

We believe in God the Father Almighty, Creator of heaven and earth.

But we also believe that God created everything through the Son. We can rightfully call Jesus our Creator and praise him for it. All that exists came from him.

He is a Creator but also Savior. He redeemed us from death and the grave.

Creator. Savior. These words are used of Yahweh, the God of Abraham, Isaac, and Jacob. They are also used of Jesus of Nazareth. Whatever God the Father promised to Israel and to the world he fulfils in his Son, the Word made flesh. So we praise, hail, and adore Jesus just as we do God the Father.

"Creator and Savior Jesus, we praise you for your greatness."

OCTOBER
1

HYMN

Praise our creator and gracious defender,

Rock where in safety we still may abide;

He is our shepherd, how gently He leads us,

Where in the valley the cool waters glide.

SCRIPTURE

For the Lamb on the throne will be their Shepherd. He will lead them to springs of life-giving water. And God will wipe every tear from their eyes (Revelation 7:17).

MEDITATION

As I write this, I am sipping on a glass of cool water. How much do we take water for granted. We just turn the tap or open a bottle and there it is. But if you have ever been in a desert climate, you know how precious water is. If you have ever been genuinely thirsty, you know what you would give for a glass of cool water.

The Lord is our Shepherd and leads us to clear waters. Jesus is the great Shepherd who waters his sheep. The day will come when we drink of the river of life.

Think of God and water. He divides the waters at creation. He judges the world in the flood. He brings life-giving water to his people from a rock. He washes us in the waters of baptism. He pours out the Spirit to refresh like water.

"Great Shepherd, lead us today to life-giving water."

OCTOBER 2

HYMN

Praise our creator, the fountain of goodness,

Now in His grandeur exalted above;

Rest in His mercy and trust in His promise,

Ever to keep us, upheld by His love.

SCRIPTURE

God blesses those who hunger and thirst for justice, for they will be satisfied (Matthew 5:6).

MEDITATION

What are you thirsty for?

We've spoken of thirst for water, but there are other thirsts and other hungers. We thirst for a kind word. For recognition. For understanding. For love.

Jesus says God blesses a thirst for justice. Do we have that thirst? Or are we comfortable with the status quo where the rich get richer, and the poor get poorer? Have we become so accustomed to injustice that we say, "That's just the way it is. Nothing will ever change"?

Older translations say those who thirst for righteousness are blessed. We may think of righteousness as being right with God, but here it means that we thirst for God to make things right in the world. God alone is the fountain of goodness, of righteousness, and of justice.

"Father, may we thirst for justice. May we bring justice to others."

OCTOBER 3

HYMN

Praise Him, praise Him,

Glory in the highest unto Him ascribing;

Praise Him, praise Him,

Blessed be His name, our Lord and king!

SCRIPTURE

Therefore, God elevated him to the place of highest honor and gave him the name above all other names (Philippians 2:9).

MEDITATION

Names do not mean much in our culture. You may know the meaning of your name, but others do not. They simply use your name as a tag for you.

In the Bible (and in some cultures today), names have meaning. Abraham means father. Isaac is laughter. Jacob is a heal-grabber. Jesus is the same name as Joshua, meaning savior. When people used these names, they thought of the meaning. There is even a name for God, Yahweh, meaning "the one who is."

When we bless the name of God or the name of Jesus, we are praising everything their name implies. We praise the God who is. We praise the one who is Savior. We exalt the name that is above all other names.

"Lord and King, we bless you name with words and deeds."

OCTOBER 4

HYMN

"Though your sins be as scarlet, Though they be red like crimson,
They shall be as white as snow; They shall be as wool!"

SCRIPTURE

Then he said to me, "These are the ones who died in the great tribulation. They have washed their robes in the blood of the Lamb and made them white" (Revelation 7:14).

MEDITATION

Ads for laundry detergent always focus on the stains they can remove. A scarlet or crimson stain on a white garment would be especially difficult to remove.

Scripture speaks of sin as a stain. Sin is not the way things were intended to be. God made his people to be stainless. But we have ruined our lives by defying the law of God.

The words of this hymn are a quotation from Isaiah 1:18. Isaiah accuses God's people of rebellion against God and of injustice to their neighbors. They continue to worship and sacrifice to God, but they will not obey. In spite of their apostasy, God is willing to completely cleanse them.

So also with us. Washed in the blood of the Lamb.

"Merciful God, wash us clean in the blood of Jesus."

OCTOBER 5

HYMN

Hear the voice that entreats you,
O return ye unto God!

He is of great compassion,
And of wondrous love.

SCRIPTURE

"Ever since the days of your ancestors, you have scorned my decrees and failed to obey them. Now return to me, and I will return to you," says the Lord of Heaven's Armies (Malachi 3:7).

MEDITATION

It is amazing to think of God entreating us. We may beg God to help us in our prayers, but here God begs us to return to him.

If you know this hymn by Fanny Crosby, then you know its power is in repetition. Four times it repeats, "Hear the voice that entreats you, O return ye unto God." That repetition reflects the numerous times in the Bible that God calls his people to return. Jesus told his followers to forgive those who sin against them seventy times seven times. God forgives us more often than that! No matter how many times we sin against him, no matter how far we wander away, no matter how stubborn our rebellion, he pleads with us to return.

God never gives up on us.

"Loving and compassionate God, draw us back to you."

OCTOBER 6

HYMN

He'll forgive your transgressions,
And remember them no more;

"Look unto Me, ye people,"
Saith the Lord your God!

SCRIPTURE

"I—yes, I alone—will blot out your sins for my own sake and will never think of them again" (Isaiah 43:25).

MEDITATION

Sometimes late at night when I'm trying to go to sleep I am plagued by memories of all the stupid things I have done. I replay the scenes of those foolish choices in my head. Not all my embarrassing acts were transgressions against God, but many of them were.

We have more trouble forgiving ourselves than God does in forgiving us. That's not the best way to put it. God's forgiveness was great trouble. It cost him his Son. But God's forgiveness is more complete than what we often give to ourselves. He forgives and forgets.

Let us also forget. Let us give up those episodes of regret to God and embrace our forgiveness, our purity, and our return to God. He sees us as his spotless beloved children. Let us see ourselves that way.

"Forgiving God, may we look to you and not look at our past sins."

OCTOBER 7

HYMN

We come again, O gracious Lord, To feast upon Thy living Word,

Around Thy hallowed mercy seat, And lay our burdens at Thy feet.

SCRIPTURE

Give your burdens to the Lord, and he will take care of you. He will not permit the godly to slip and fall (Psalm 55:22).

MEDITATION

"I can't take this anymore!"

We've all felt that and said that. The load that life places on us seems too much to carry. There are family burdens. Your daughter has a child. The father is nowhere to be found. The responsibility of raising that child falls on you. You feel too old to go back to feedings and changings and worry. There are work burdens. You get a promotion only to find that they expect you to do your old job alongside the new one.

Sometimes it's a little thing that is the straw that breaks the camel's back. The refrigerator breaks at the same time as the washer. If only there could be a week without a crisis!

When we cannot take it anymore, we bring it to the one who carries the load with us.

"Gracious Lord, we lay our burdens at your feet."

OCTOBER 8

HYMN

We come again, for still we need
Refreshing showers our hearts to cheer,
In Thy dear name the grace we plead,
That to Thy throne will bring us near.

SCRIPTURE

I will bless my people and their homes around my holy hill. And in the proper season I will send the showers they need. There will be showers of blessing (Ezekiel 34:26).

MEDITATION

I love a good shower. It is amazing to me that God made us to where we can gain such pleasure from getting clean.

Of course, the showers mentioned here are even more important. They are rain showers that make the crops grow so we can eat and live.

Both types of showers are refreshing. They make everything new and fresh. When we spend time with God in prayer we let go of our burdens. He gives us a fresh start in life, He renews us through his grace, giving us the strength to carry on. Time with God is like a daily shower, like a reinvigorating rain. God does not dribble out his blessings but enlivens us with his gushing love.

"Father, pour your blessings on us today."

OCTOBER 9

HYMN

Our strength renew, our hope increase,

And may we now Thy blessings share;

Keep Thou Thine own in perfect peace,

Control our thoughts, direct our prayer.

SCRIPTURE

You will keep in perfect peace all who trust in you, all whose thoughts are fixed on you! (Isaiah 26:3).

MEDITATION

We live in an age of anxiety. Twenty-four hour news bombards us with new reasons to worry. We have our near concerns—family, work, finances, and more. Then the troubles of the world—famine, war, and injustice—hit us. We find it hard to have peaceful thoughts.

In those times of unease and fear, we come to the source of calm and comfort—the Prince of Peace. We cast our thoughts on the God who is in control. We focus on a Father who lovingly provides. We center on a Savior who lives to intercede for us. We experience the Spirit who helps us. We encounter the God of all comfort.

In that time alone with God, our troubles do not always disappear but they are swallowed up in the vision of his majesty and character.

"Peace-giving God, calm our hearts in your Presence."

OCTOBER 10

HYMN

And when this hour shall pass away,

Oh, may Thy presence come so near

That from our hearts we all may say,

'Twas good for us to gather here.

SCRIPTURE

And let us not neglect our meeting together, as some people do, but encourage one another, especially now that the day of his return is drawing near (Hebrews 10:25).

MEDITATION

Time alone with God is precious. The time we spend with others in prayer and praise is even more so.

"Church" has fallen on hard times lately. Some find it boring and irrelevant. Even some who consider themselves good Christians see no need to meet regularly with other believers.

But we need other flesh-and-blood Christians to encourage us. Being a disciple of Jesus is difficult. We believe strange things. We believe in a God of love in spite of the way things look in our world. We need others around us who also believe these things.

And we are not meeting with them alone. We are meeting with God. Father, Son, and Spirit are there with us as church. So we say, it is good to gather here.

"Lord, may we know your presence in the assembly of your holy people."

OCTOBER 11

HYMN

Shut out the world, that we may see

Within our midst no one but Thee;

Our love inspire through faith divine,

That we may hear no voice but Thine.

SCRIPTURE

Your own ears will hear him. Right behind you a voice will say, "This is the way you should go," whether to the right or to the left (Isaiah 30:21).

MEDITATION

Surrounded by the noise of competing voices, it is hard to hear a clear word from God. That's why we need to set aside a time to shut out the noise and listen to God alone. It is also why we need to listen to his voice with others.

We may be suspicious of those who claim to hear the voice of God. We have our own suspicions that we might be confusing what we want with what we think we hear from God. But we trust that God speaks. And we test what we hear through others who are listening to his voice.

To go through life not listening for God would be tragic. We would be subject to the many voices that tell us how to live. Thank God, he speaks! And he wants us to listen and to obey.

"God who speaks, open the ears of our hearts to listen."

OCTOBER 12

HYMN

Speak not harshly when reproving
Those from duty's path who stray;
If we would reclaim the erring
Kindness must each action sway.

SCRIPTURE

Dear brothers and sisters, if another believer is overcome by some sin, you who are godly should gently and humbly help that person back onto the right path. And be careful not to fall into the same temptation yourself (Galatians 6:1).

MEDITATION

Some accuse Christians of being judgmental, harsh, and hypocritical. We must admit that sometimes these accusations are true.

Jesus clearly teaches us not to judge. That does not mean that we do not stand against evil and injustice. It does mean that we make that stand with humility and understanding.

We must forcibly condemn hatred, unfairness, and prejudice. But we do it with gentleness and kindness. We have empathy with those who are weak and broken. We are weak and broken ourselves. And we must not practice the things we so loudly condemn. There is no place for pretense.

"Just God, may we leave judgment to you. Give us the love to keep from harsh speech."

OCTOBER
13

HYMN

Speak not harshly to the wayward—
They will feel how pure the motive

Win their confidence—their love;
That hath led us to reprove.

SCRIPTURE

They must not slander anyone and must avoid quarreling. Instead, they should be gentle and show true humility to everyone (Titus 3:2).

MEDITATION

There is a fine but clear line between helping someone see their faults and feeling superior because our faults are somehow not as bad. Jesus does condemn judging, but he also says to judge others the way we want to be judged (Matthew 7:2).

How do I want to be judged? With generosity. When I cut you off when driving in traffic, I want you to know that I did not do it on purpose. It was just a mistake. How do I want to be judged? With mercy. When I cut you off on purpose, I want forgiveness. Please cut me some slack.

But if you cut me off, I'll shout and blow my horn, knowing you meant to harm me.

How would Jesus drive? With grace, mercy, and pure motives.

"Lord Jesus, purify our hearts so we may correct others the way we want correction."

OCTOBER 14

HYMN

Speak not harshly to the stranger,
Thou he come in humble guise;

Think how slight a thing would kindle
Gladness in a stranger's eyes.

SCRIPTURE

Since God chose you to be the holy people he loves, you must clothe yourselves with tenderhearted mercy, kindness, humility, gentleness, and patience (Colossians 3:12).

MEDITATION

"You know what *they* are like."

"They" being those who are strange, not like us. They may be foreigners who talk funny. They may be young people with their tattoos and piercings. They may be old people who dress in old fashion styles. They may be those who support the other political party. Why can't they be normal like us?

But what if we are "they"? What if we are the stranger, the outsider, the oddball? Then we want others to understand and accept us as we are. We want gentle and kind words.

So we should go out of our way to speak kindly to "them." They too are beloved children of God. He sent his Son for them.

"Father, may we show your love to those we find strange."

OCTOBER
15

HYMN

Speak not harshly to the felon,
Though like adamant his heart;
Touch one chord of fond affection,
And the scalding tear may start.

SCRIPTURE

Remember those in prison, as if you were there yourself. Remember also those being mistreated, as if you felt their pain in your own bodies (Hebrews 13:3).

MEDITATION

Not speaking harshly to a criminal may sound sentimental and naïve. If only we were nice to them, they would end their life of crime.

But Fanny Crosby was not uncritical and inexperienced when it came to felons. She spent much of her life helping those in the Rescue Missions of New York City, many of whom were hardened criminals. She knew from experience that the hardest heart can be touched by kindness.

Many churches today help released criminals. They do so knowing that they must set boundaries and have clear expectations. But they also know that kind and gentle words and actions are what these former felons need most.

To remember those in prison is to care for them there and when they get out.

"Lord Jesus who sets the prisoners free, give us wisdom and compassion."

OCTOBER 16

HYMN

Speak not harshly to the orphan, / They have borne of grief their share;

Add not to their heavy burden, / Add not to corroding care.

SCRIPTURE

Pure and genuine religion in the sight of God the Father means caring for orphans and widows in their distress and refusing to let the world corrupt you (James 1:27).

MEDITATION

A couple in our church has adopted three special needs children from other countries.

"How sweet," you might say. But a shallow sentiment will not care for those three kids. Each child has unique challenges. Their parents have no off days or even off times. During church these kids are often loud and disruptive. I am in awe of their parents' skill in correcting them firmly but gently.

Yet those children are not a disruption or distraction to our worship. Our whole church has embraced them as our children. When they are quiet, we miss their voices. We teach them, listen to them, play with them, and are gladdened by their smiles. They are a blessing to us all.

Their parents, who constantly care for them, would say the same.

"Jesus who called children to him, give us strength to love orphans."

OCTOBER 17

HYMN

Speak not harshly, was the precept

Which to man the Savior taught—

May that precept ever guide us—

Gentle words will cost us naught.

SCRIPTURE

Take my yoke upon you. Let me teach you, because I am humble and gentle at heart, and you will find rest for your souls (Matthew 11:29).

MEDITATION

Jesus sometimes spoke harsh words.

But he spoke harsh words only to those who needed him to shout so they could hear him. He never shouted at those physically hard-of-hearing but to those who closed the ears of their hearts to him--Pharisees, Bible experts, and prideful priests. He spoke harshly out of love, trying to convince them that they needed his spiritual healing.

To those who knew they were fragile and broken—the sick, the tax collectors, the prostitutes, and the poor—his words were gentle and accepting. He bound up the wounded. He gave hope to those in despair. He carried the load of the over-burdened.

He calls us to the same gentleness.

"Understanding Jesus, keep us from speaking harshly to the vulnerable."

OCTOBER 18

HYMN

O my Savior, I am weary!
Let my cry to Thee ascend

While in humble supplication
Now before Thy throne I bend!

SCRIPTURE

Be merciful to me, O Lord, for I am calling on you constantly (Psalm 86:3).

MEDITATION

Many people I know are weary to their bones. They live in constant fatigue. Days off from work do not help. Weekends seem busier than workdays with house chores, soccer games, and paying bills. Vacations are not times of rest but of stress. We need a vacation to recover from the vacation!

The weariness we feel may be more than the result of our busy lives. We can grow tired of life itself, wondering what it is all about.

In that life of exhaustion, we need a strength and rest that comes from a source beyond the grind of this world. We need to turn to the one who knows what it is like to be weary, one who sought vigor from his Father in prayer. We bend before the throne of Jesus, our Savior, trusting that he hears our cry for renewal.

"Savior, give us rest and life this day."

OCTOBER 19

HYMN

O my Savior, tho' unworthy,

I have nowhere else to go;

Thou canst pardon my transgressions,

Thou canst wash me white as snow!

SCRIPTURE

Then Jesus turned to the Twelve and asked, "Are you also going to leave?" Simon Peter replied, "Lord, to whom would we go? You have the words that give eternal life" (John 6:67-68).

MEDITATION

One thing that keeps me from a greater dependence on God is a lack of desperation. I have never known real hunger. I've been sick, but never near death. I have all my limbs and my senses. I've experience little violence or even ridicule. When I do have trouble, I can depend on my bank account or doctors or counselors to help me get through it.

By contrast, the desperate came to Jesus. A man born blind. A woman with seven demons. A detested tax collector. All came to Jesus because they had nowhere else to go. And Jesus healed, forgave, and even called them to discipleship.

We should not ask for trouble. But we need to remember the one source of our healing, pardon, and life.

"Jesus, giver of eternal life, make us more desperate for you."

OCTOBER
20

HYMN

O my Savior, by Thy Spirit
Thou hast called me o'er and o'er;
Now repentant I am coming;
Lord, my wand'ring soul restore!

SCRIPTURE

God will make this happen, for he who calls you is faithful (1 Thessalonians 5:24).

MEDITATION

Jesus calls us. We are his disciples. We heard his call and followed. We joyfully recall that day, that moment when we responded to the call and gave our life to him.

He still calls us. But we get distracted, sometimes by sin. We follow our own path instead of listening to the one who guides us. Sometimes good things distract us. We get so caught up in the enjoyment of our blessings that we fail to pay attention to the one who blesses.

Jesus is always calling. Are we listening?

What does it take to listen? It takes effort. It takes discipline. It takes the regular practice of spending time alone with God—Father, Son, and Spirit. When we do that, God restores our wandering soul.

"Jesus, through your Spirit, open the ears of our hearts to listen this day."

OCTOBER 21

HYMN

O my Savior, do not leave me

Here to perish at Thy throne;

In Thy tender, loving mercy

Cleanse and make me all Thine own!

SCRIPTURE

Wash me clean from my guilt. Purify me from my sin (Psalm 51:2).

MEDITATION

Stains. We see them on our clothes, on the carpet, and in the car. If you look for them, they are everywhere—lampshades, walls, and windows. Weeds and disease stain our grass. Our skin is stained by zits, moles, and spots. Our world is filled with stains. So many things leave a mark or blemish.

Worst of all are those inner blotches that smudge us. Regrets, grudges, and (to use the biblical word) sins. Guilt and shame stain us.

At the risk of sounding like an infomercial, there is a miracle stain remover. At the throne of Jesus, we receive complete cleansing. All stains, blemishes, regrets, shame and guilt are gone permanently! Jesus sanitizes us with his righteousness. He sets us clean and fresh before the throne of God.

"Lord Jesus, be merciful to us as sinners! Make us completely clean in your sight."

OCTOBER 22

HYMN

Weak and helpless, yet believing, / I am hoping, trusting, praying;

Casting all my care on Thee, / Have compassion, Lord, on me!

SCRIPTURE

So the Lord must wait for you to come to him so he can show you his love and compassion. For the Lord is a faithful God. Blessed are those who wait for his help (Isaiah 30:18).

MEDITATION

We struggle all our lives to be good enough. Good enough to pass the test. Good enough to make the team. Good enough to be hired. Good enough for the promotion. Sadly, some struggle to be loved and accepted by parents, spouse, children, and friends.

I was never quite good enough. My guess is that you also were not good enough.

The great good news is that God does not wait for us to be good enough. I've known many who said, "I'll start coming to church when I get my life straightened out." But God is not waiting for us to straighten everything out before he accepts us. He is waiting to show us his compassion, his complete acceptance. All he asks is that we cast our cares, our inadequacies, on him. He wants to show us his love. Will we let him?

"Lord, may we keep you waiting no longer. Have compassion on us!"

OCTOBER
23

HYMN

This life is a garden where action and deed

May spring into gladness by sowing the seed;

God give us abundantly sunshine and show'rs,

And we may have brambles, or beautiful flow'rs.

SCRIPTURE

Jesus also said, "The Kingdom of God is like a farmer who scatters seed on the ground. Night and day, while he's asleep or awake, the seed sprouts and grows, but he does not understand how it happens" (Mark 4:26-27).

MEDITATION

I planted some Morning Glory seeds the other day. The day after I planted them, I went out to look at them. Nothing was happening. Of course! It takes time for plants to grow. Watching does not hasten the process. If we give plants too much water or fertilizer in hopes of speeding their growth, it can kill the plant.

Growing takes time. It requires patience.

So also with the kingdom of God. It is God's kingdom, and he grows it in mysterious ways. But we can trust his power to bring great plants from small seeds. What he asks of us is to follow him as disciples and plant the seed.

"God of growth, may your love spring up in our lives this day."

OCTOBER 24

HYMN

The kindness to others, which all may bestow, Will blossom for heaven from seed which we sow;

SCRIPTURE

"The earth produces the crops on its own. First a leaf blade pushes through, then the heads of wheat are formed, and finally the grain ripens." (Mark 4:28).

MEDITATION

What does it mean to sow or plant the seed that grows into the kingdom of God? I was taught that sowing the seed meant evangelism and that evangelism meant putting in a good word for Jesus.

However, for an introvert like me, putting in a good word for Jesus makes me feel self-conscious and disingenuous. It looks like steering conversations to "spiritual" matters in order to manipulate people.

We plant the seed best when we genuinely exhibit the fruit of the Spirit in our lives. We should be more concerned with growing in the Spirit than in convincing others about Jesus. Seeing the fruit of the Spirit in us will plant the seed of the good news of Jesus in their hearts.

"Holy Spirit, produce your fruit in me so that others may glorify God."

OCTOBER
25

HYMN

The words of salvation for lost ones will be A crown of rejoicing for you and for me.

SCRIPTURE

"And as soon as the grain is ready, the farmer comes and harvests it with a sickle, for the harvest time has come" (Mark 4:29).

MEDITATION

Planting takes effort. Waiting takes more effort. I wait for my flowers to grow and bloom. It seems to take forever. But if (like most people in the world) I had to wait not for flowers but for crops so I and my family could eat and live, then the waiting would be more excruciating.

We wait for the kingdom to come. At times it seems it never will. We cannot force the kingdom to come, but we wait in trust and hope.

Our job is to plant and wait. But there comes another job, the joyful task of harvest. Harvesting is hard work, but we labor joyfully knowing that we and those we love will eat and live. We plant, we wait, and we pray "Your kingdom come, your will be done on earth as it is in heaven." We pray, knowing that the great harvest is coming. We may plant in pain and sorrow. We may live many days in expectation. But we know the harvest festival is coming.

"Lord of the harvest, may we wait in patient hope for your gifts."

OCTOBER 26

HYMN

O we must be careful of seed that we sow,

Uprooting the weeds from the soil where they grow;

We'll need to keep praying as onward we press,

And asking the Savior our efforts to bless.

SCRIPTURE

Jesus said, "How can I describe the Kingdom of God? What story should I use to illustrate it? It is like a mustard seed planted in the ground" (Mark 4:30).

MEDITATION

"Our thoughts and prayers are with you."

That phrase can infuriate us because we know it comes from those who have the power to help but refuse to do so. Their "thoughts and prayers" are empty because they refuse to show compassion.

On the other hand, there are those I love dearly, but the only thing I can do for them is to pray for them. They will not accept my money, advice, or even work on their behalf. Praying for them is not "the only thing" I can do for them. It is the most important thing. Yes, we show justice and compassion, but our work for others is always accompanied by our profoundly felt appeal to our Savior to bless them.

"Giving Jesus, we cry to you to care for those we love this day."

OCTOBER 27

HYMN

We'll scatter good seed in word and in deed,

And Jesus will bless it, we know;

In mercy and love, for heaven above,

We'll scatter good seed as we go.

SCRIPTURE

"It is the smallest of all seeds, but it becomes the largest of all garden plants; it grows long branches, and birds can make nests in its shade" (Mark 4:31-32).

MEDITATION

We admire Christians who have done great things for God. We stand in awe of those who plant churches, convert hundreds, and feed thousands.

But that admiration can make us feel inadequate. I've known Christians who say, "I'd like to be more involved at church, to do more for Jesus, but I'm too busy raising four children." Or they are too busy caring for their older parents or too busy running a business that employs dozens or too busy teaching a classroom full of kids.

Yet, by doing those tasks for Jesus, they are planting seeds. Jesus does not call us to great deeds but to daily "mustard-seed" discipleship. The small acts we do, even if it is giving a cup of cold water in his name, will be rewarded beyond our imagination.

"As we go today, Lord, may we scatter small seeds of mercy and love."

OCTOBER 28

HYMN

Thou only art holy,
Thou only the Lord;
Truth, mercy and judgment,
Shine forth in Thy Word.

SCRIPTURE

"Who will not fear you, Lord, and glorify your name? For you alone are holy. All nations will come and worship before you, for your righteous deeds have been revealed" (Revelation 15:4).

MEDITATION

"Holy." It's a word I struggle to comprehend.

Holy means God is great, and God is good. The Lord alone is holy. He is unique (an overused word). There is no one like him. What does it mean for us to confess that God alone is holy? It means he is God, and we are not. More than that, it means he alone is good. We are not holy. We are fallen, broken, and sinful. We are not the way God made us to be. We have gone our own way, not his way.

The good news is that the Lord makes us holy. He shares his nature with us, filling us with his goodness. And the day will come when all will see his holiness shining forth in his word.

"Holy Lord, make all the nations and people holy."

OCTOBER 29

HYMN

Thou rulest and reignest
All others above;
Thy throne is eternal,
Thy scepter is love.

SCRIPTURE

Your throne, O God, endures forever and ever. You rule with a scepter of justice (Psalm 45:6).

MEDITATION

I have been to Buckingham Palace and seen the throne room of the king. It is spectacular.

Where is the throne room of God? The Most Holy Place in the tabernacle and in the temple was the throne room of God. There on top of the Ark of the Covenant was the Mercy Seat—the throne of God. The name itself shows how God rules his people, not with power alone but with mercy and love.

Of course, the Most Holy Place did not contain God. He is everywhere. Other Bible verses speak of heaven as his throne. That does not mean he reigns from the sky but that the expanse of the universe cannot contain him. If the throne room of a limited earthly king is spectacular, how much more majestic is the throne room of God.

The Holy God rules over all.

"Almighty King, we bow before your throne this day. Have mercy on us!"

OCTOBER
30

HYMN

Thou only art holy;   Thy laws are unchanging,

In Thee is our trust;   Thy statutes are just.

SCRIPTURE

The commandments of the Lord are right, bringing joy to the heart. The commands of the Lord are clear, giving insight for living (Psalm 19:8).

MEDITATION

I have never been a fan of rules, regulations, and requirements. Obeying commands might be necessary at times, but keeping commandments does not bring joy to my heart.

But the Psalmist often expresses gratitude for the Lord's commandments, laws, and statutes. Perhaps my problem is with language. I feel better about words such as direction, guideline, and instruction than I do about "law." The holy God gives us his loving guidance so that we might live holy, just, and joyous lives. Obeying him might sometime be difficult for us, but it is easier knowing that he is not making up arbitrary rules but providing guidance for the good life.

And when we don't understand the reason for his commands, we trust.

"Holy God, teach us how to live today."

OCTOBER 31

HYMN

All nations and people
Before Thee shall fall;
The Father, Redeemer,
And Savior of all.

SCRIPTURE

All the nations you made will come and bow before you, Lord; they will praise your holy name (Psalm 86:9).

MEDITATION

The kingdom of God exists through space and time. "Through space and time" may sound like a line from a Star Trek film, but it reminds us of the expanse of God's rule. The boundaries of God's kingdom encompass all nations and all people. Space, that is, distance cannot separate us from our brothers and sisters in Christ.

So when we celebrate the Lord's Supper with our local assembly of disciples, we are also communing with those far away. When I worship here in the United States, I think of those I know in other lands—Japan, Korea, Australia, India, Zimbabwe, Brazil and elsewhere. I have shared the bread and cup with them in person. Now I continue to share it with them from a distance. God's kingdom encompasses the planet.

"God who rules all nations, give us love for neighbors near and far."

NOVEMBER 1

HYMN

Thou only art holy;
The angels in light

With prophets and martyrs
Their anthems unite.

SCRIPTURE

And from the throne came a voice that said, "Praise our God, all his servants, all who fear him, from the least to the greatest" (Revelation 19:5).

MEDITATION

The kingdom of God exists not only through space, but through time. Just as distance cannot truly separate us from our fellow believers, so time cannot separate us. We are one with all those followers of Jesus who have gone before us. Even death cannot detach us from the saints, the holy ones of God, because they have gone to be with the Lord.

Traditionally, this date is All Saints Day. It is a day set aside to help us remember those Christians who have gone before us and passed the faith down to us. They may be those close to us in time--those who personally taught us of Jesus--or they may be far removed in time—those who shaped us through their writing or through a chain of spiritual heritage.

We join with prophets, martyrs, and ordinary saints to praise our Savior.

"Father, thank you for those who shaped our faith and now are with you."

NOVEMBER 2

HYMN

Thou only art holy,   The boundless creation

O Ancient of days;   Is filled with Thy praise.

SCRIPTURE

I watched as thrones were put in place and the Ancient One sat down to judge. His clothing was as white as snow, his hair like purest wool. He sat on a fiery throne with wheels of blazing fire (Daniel 7:9).

MEDITATION

I've sometimes jokingly referred to some of my older friends as "ancient of days."

The Bible uses the phrase to speak of God. Ancient of Days does not mean that he is old and decrepit. He is not the way he is sometimes pictured, as an old bearded guy in the sky who is out of touch with reality. Ancient of Days does not mean he is aged but that he is timeless.

A Timeless God. He existed before there was time. He will be God when time will be no more. He created time. He rules time. He lives outside time but out of love enters time to create, to become incarnate, to save.

We cannot imagine anything outside time. But we can worship the One who is.

"Timeless God, may we trust your love which time cannot change."

NOVEMBER 3

HYMN

Thy reign everlasting,   Henceforth and forever

Thy kingdom divine,   All glory be Thine.

SCRIPTURE

For your kingdom is an everlasting kingdom. You rule throughout all generations (Psalm 145:13).

MEDITATION

The kingdom of God. We read that phase often in the Bible, but what does it mean?

"Kingdom" brings to mind a country with boundaries led by a king. We had a king in America but got rid of him quickly. Most kings today rule democracies where their power is limited. Only a few kings in our time have complete authority over their country.

What about the kingdom of God? What are its boundaries? Surely God reigns over all creation; there are no limits to his authority. Yet not everyone and not every nation accepts his rule. They have been deceived by a usurper, Satan. He fools us into thinking we are in charge.

God reminds his people that he rules all and he rules forever. And so we pray, "your kingdom come." We pray for the day when everyone acknowledges his reign.

"Sovereign God, we bow before you as our king. May every knee bow."

NOVEMBER 4

HYMN

Thou my everlasting portion,   All along my pilgrim journey,

more than friend or life to me,   Savior, let me walk with Thee.

SCRIPTURE

Instead of shame and dishonor, you will enjoy a double share of honor. You will possess a double portion of prosperity in your land, and everlasting joy will be yours (Isaiah 61:7).

MEDITATION

"I just want my fair share." That is a noble sentiment. We are not greedy, demanding more than we deserve. We only want what is rightfully ours.

When Israel entered the Promised Land, the Lord allotted each tribe and each family their portion of land. It was to be their land forever. But many in Israel forgot their covenant with God. They lost their land and were sent into exile. But God promises a restoration of Israel where they will not only recover their land but get a double portion. The Lord gives more than what they deserve, more than their fair share.

This hymn points us to our true treasure. Not land, but a Savior. He is our portion. If we walk with him daily, we will have everlasting joy.

"Jesus, our Savior, may you be more than friend or life to us."

NOVEMBER 5

HYMN

Not for ease or worldly pleasure, / nor for fame my prayer shall be; / Gladly will I toil and suffer, / only let me walk with Thee.

SCRIPTURE

Then he said to the crowd, "If any of you wants to be my follower, you must give up your own way, take up your cross daily, and follow me" (Luke 9:23).

MEDITATION

Everybody wants to be somebody. We want to be noticed. We want to count for something. We want others to look up to us.

Many try to be somebody through fame. We identify with famous people, even idolize them. We imitate them in hope that their fame rubs off on us.

Or we give up trying to be somebody and settle for taking it easy. If we can make enough money, we can enjoy a good life.

Jesus makes us somebody. Through him God adopts us as his beloved children. Jesus gives us rest and genuine joy. All he asks is that we walk with him each day. Yet we must learn that if we walk with him, he will lead us to glory through the path of the cross.

"May we gladly suffer with you, Jesus, so we might be your somebodies."

NOVEMBER 6

HYMN

Lead me through the vale of shadows,

bear me over life's fitful sea;

Then the gate of life eternal may I enter, Lord, with Thee.

SCRIPTURE

When everything is ready, I will come and get you, so that you will always be with me where I am (John 14:3).

MEDITATION

Of course, if suffering were the only word we heard from Jesus, we would be fools to follow him. But the last word is not death but life.

I have often struggled against the "heaven talk" I have heard in church. Some of it sounds greedy. "I want the biggest and gaudiest mansion in heaven." Some of it is an excuse not to fight against the injustices we see around us. "That's just the way it is; there's nothing we can do about it. Our job is just to hold out until heaven."

Yet life is the last word. Eternal life. Knowing that God will make everything right in the new heaven and earth gives us the strength to fight for justice now in the face of overwhelming odds. It gives us the hope to survive the sea of troubles.

"Lord, protect us as we suffer for the sake of others, so we may enter life with you."

NOVEMBER

HYMN

Close to Thee, close to Thee, All along my pilgrim journey,

close to Thee, close to Thee, Savior, let me walk with Thee.

SCRIPTURE

But the people of God will sing a song of joy, like the songs at the holy festivals. You will be filled with joy, as when a flutist leads a group of pilgrims to Jerusalem, the mountain of the Lord— to the Rock of Israel (Isaiah 30:29).

MEDITATION

Perhaps you have been on a religious pilgrimage. That entails flying to another state or country, meeting with a group, then sometimes walking a great distance over several days to a pilgrimage site. The site itself has a history as a "thin place," a place where there is little distance between heaven and earth, a place where one encounters God.

Israelites made their pilgrimage from their homes to Jerusalem to worship at the great feasts. That also required long days of walking. Though it was tiring, they sang joyous songs as they went, knowing they would encounter the Lord.

Our life is a pilgrimage, a long and tiring walk. But we encounter the Lord along the way.

"Jesus, keep us close to you in our walk of life."

NOVERMBER
8

HYMN

Praise ye the Lord, the hope of our salvation;

Praise ye the Lord, our soul's abiding trust;

SCRIPTURE

I pray that God, the source of hope, will fill you completely with joy and peace because you trust in him. Then you will overflow with confident hope through the power of the Holy Spirit (Romans 15:13).

MEDITATION

"I hope it rains today."

That is a sincere hope. We are in the middle of heat and drought. I use the word "hope" to mean something like, "That would be a nice or a helpful thing to happen."

In the Bible, hope is a much more vigorous word. Our hope is not in circumstances, but in the certainty of trust in God. The Lord has promised us full salvation. He will make everything right. Our hope is not optimism based on trends we see but certainty based on the character of God.

So we fervently praise the Lord who guarantees our hope.

"Trustworthy God, tune our hearts to hope in you alone."

NOVEMBER 9

HYMN

Great are His works   Praise ye the Lord,

and wonderful His counsels;   the only wise and just.

SCRIPTURE

All glory to the only wise God, through Jesus Christ, forever. Amen (Romans 16:27).

MEDITATION

What does it mean to be wise?

In a world of experts, life hacks, and an abundance of advice, we may think of wisdom as a technique. But it is much more than that. Wisdom is knowing how to live. It includes the ability to anticipate the consequences of our actions. The wise see clearer and farther than others can see.

There is one who is All-Seeing. The Lord is the source of all wisdom. The Creator who gave us life knows how we should live life to the fullest. And he shares that secret of abundance with us! All he asks us to do is to trust his counsel. God is the ultimate expert whose advice is beyond all price and yet is free. His wisdom leads us to justice for all.

Praise the wise and just Lord!

"God of all understanding, enlighten us this day."

NOVEMBER
10

HYMN

Praise ye the Lord, our Strength and our Redeemer,

Praise ye the Lord, His mighty love recall,

Tell how He came from bondage to deliver,

Tell how He came to purchase life for all.

SCRIPTURE

Don't you realize that your body is the temple of the Holy Spirit, who lives in you and was given to you by God? You do not belong to yourself, for God bought you with a high price. So you must honor God with your body (1 Corinthians 6:19-20).

MEDITATION

How much would you give to ransom someone you love from kidnapping? Surely, we'd give everything we own. What would we give to ransom ourselves? Every penny we have. That money would do us no good if we were dead.

How much did God give to ransom us from Satan who had us in his power? All that he had. He gave his only Son.

God bought us back from Satan. Jesus purchased us with his own life. We therefore doubly belong to God. He made us. We are his. He redeemed us. He paid the price to receive what was rightfully his. He lives in our bodies through the Spirit.

"God of love, may we honor you this day as the one who bought us."

NOVEMBER 11

HYMN

Praise ye the Lord, whose throne is everlasting;

Praise ye the Lord, whose gifts are ever new;

SCRIPTURE

God has given each of you a gift from his great variety of spiritual gifts. Use them well to serve one another (1 Peter 4:10).

MEDITATION

Have you ever been called "gifted"? Perhaps you are a gifted student or athlete or writer. We associate "gifted" with natural, inborn abilities.

But when the Bible speaks of gifts, it refers not to natural talents but to a supernatural outpouring of ability from God. God may give that at birth, but often his gifts come later, through the Spirit, God's greatest gift.

And gifts require effort. Gifted students have to study hard. Gifted athletes put in hours of practice. Gifted writers have to write when they don't feel like it. But no matter how hard we work to use God's gifts to bless others, we praise him for those ever-new gifts. And we accept those free gifts with gratitude and wonder.

"Giving God, we praise you for the new presents you entrust to us."

NOVEMBER
12

HYMN

Praise ye the Lord, whose tender mercy falleth

Pure as the rain and gentle as the dew.

Praise ye the Lord, oh, glory hallelujah!

SCRIPTURE

Let my teaching fall on you like rain; let my speech settle like dew. Let my words fall like rain on tender grass, like gentle showers on young plants (Deuteronomy 32:2).

MEDITATION

In the coolness of November, I think back to the long dry summer. I remember longing and praying for the cooling rain. When the rain finally came, I sat on my porch feeling the breeze and smelling the freshness.

Our Lord is a refreshing God. Yes, he is the Almighty God who appears to his people in thunder and storm. But he is also the God who knows how fragile we are and gently showers his mercy on us.

That mercy falls on us through his teaching and words. He is not a harsh, demanding God who burdens us with rules. He is the one who speaks tenderly to us, enticing us to have a deeper relationship with him. He makes his delicate plants to grow.

"Tenderhearted God, refresh us with your words this day."

NOVEMBER 13

HYMN

Praise ye the Lord, whose kingdom has no end;

Praise ye the Lord, who watcheth o'er the faithful,

Praise ye the Lord, our never changing Friend.

SCRIPTURE

And so it happened just as the Scriptures say: "Abraham believed God, and God counted him as righteous because of his faith." He was even called the friend of God (James 2:23).

MEDITATION

"I am a friend of God."

I don't think I've ever heard anyone say that. It sounds presumptuous, even sacrilegious to say. Calling God our friend puts us on the same level as he is. But he is God. We are not.

Yet God is willing to call us his friends. Jesus calls his followers "friends" (John 15:14). Does that mean we are on the same level as the Son of God? Yes, that's precisely what it means. God has adopted us as his children, made us his heirs, and called us his beloved.

This does not make us less respectful of God, but more. It does not make us proud but grateful. We praise our ever faithful Friend, the Lord God Almighty.

"Father, may we think of ourselves as your friends this day."

NOVEMBER
14

HYMN

Praise ye the Lord, for good it is to praise Him;

O let the earth His majesty proclaim;

Shout, shout for joy and bow the knee before Him;

Sing to the harp and magnify His name.

SCRIPTURE

Praise him for his mighty works; praise his unequaled greatness! Praise him with a blast of the ram's horn; praise him with the lyre and harp! (Psalm 150:2-3).

MEDITATION

There are many places in the Bible where God's people sing praise to him. When we lift our voices in song, we use words of gratitude, loyalty, and surrender to the Lord.

But singing is sometimes not enough to express our joy and praise. We shout! Sometimes our praise demands a full band—horns and harps and cymbals!

The point here is not what instruments, if any, we use to blast out our praise. We use only one instrument to genuinely bless the Lord. We use our heart. Heartfelt joyous praise bursts from our lips. Our whole bodies cry out to the One worthy of all glory. We lose ourselves in the moment of oneness with our Redeemer. We join with other believers and with all creation to magnify the name of the Lord. How good it is to praise Him!

"May we shout, sing, and make a joyful noise to you, our God."

NOVEMBER 15

HYMN

Hold Thou my hand; so weak I am, and helpless, I dare not take one step without Thy aid;

SCRIPTURE

Though they stumble, they will never fall, for the Lord holds them by the hand (Psalm 37:24).

MEDITATION

I don't remember my dad holding my hand and helping me to learn to walk, although I'm sure he did that. I do remember dad running beside me on my bicycle as I was learning to ride without training wheels. He ran, holding to the bike to give me confidence until he let go and I was riding by myself.

I wonder if God does something like that. Yes, he holds our hand to help us to walk. He makes sure we do not stumble and fall. But at some point, he lets go so we can walk on our own. Yet even then we are not on our own, although it may feel that way. God continues to protect.

Remember when your child first learned to walk. The steps were hesitant and awkward. After a few steps, they began to fall, and you caught them. Did you punish them for falling? Of course not! You shared in the joy of their attempt. So also with us and God.

"Gentle Father, hold our hands as we try to walk this day."

NOVEMBER
16

HYMN

Hold Thou my hand;

for then, O loving Savior,

No dread of ill

shall make my soul afraid.

SCRIPTURE

For I hold you by your right hand— I, the Lord your God. And I say to you, "Don't be afraid. I am here to help you" (Isaiah 41:13).

MEDITATION

We live in an age of fear.

I saw a headline on my phone, "Something is in your house that can kill you overnight." When I clicked on the story, I read that I had to pay a subscription fee to read it. Now, if there is something in my house that can kill me overnight, shouldn't the news tell me without my paying? The "news" tries to scare us so we will read their stories and buy the products they advertise. Politicians scare us to get our votes. Even those close to us sometimes manipulate us through fear.

That is not to say that there are no real dangers. That's why the most frequent command in the Bible is "Do not be afraid."

"Loving Savior, keep us from fear, knowing that you are here to help us."

NOVEMBER 17

HYMN

Hold Thou my hand, and closer, closer draw me

To Thy dear self my hope, my joy, my all;

SCRIPTURE

But the person who is joined to the Lord is one spirit with him (1 Corinthians 6:17).

MEDITATION

How do we know we are growing closer to the Lord?

Is it that we feel closer? But we have little control of our feelings. It is wonderful to feel close to Jesus, but feelings can lead us astray.

Is it that we have a profound mystical experience? I know those who say that being silent for a week or fasting for a month has changed their whole lives. I do not doubt that is true. But we can spend our lives chasing experiences and still not be closer to Jesus.

We know we are closer by faith. We trust that Jesus wants to be closer to us. The more time we spend alone with him, the more time we adore our God, and the more time we let the Spirit produce his fruit in us, the closer God draws us into his life.

"Draw us nearer to your heart this day, O Lord."

NOVEMBER 18

HYMN

Hold Thou my hand, / lest haply I should wander, / And, missing Thee, / my trembling feet should fall

SCRIPTURE

If you think you are standing strong, be careful not to fall (1 Corinthians 10:12).

MEDITATION

I do not think some dramatic event will cause me to turn my back on God. I do think that the greatest challenge to my faith is that life is so daily. Following Jesus is (in the words of Eugene Peterson) "A long obedience in the same direction."

Today looks like yesterday and tomorrow will likely look the same. It is easy to drift away from God. We do not intentionally turn our backs, but we thoughtlessly wander from the path where he leads. We walk through life blindly. We need someone to hold our hand and guide us.

Having a daily time alone with God does not make him show up. He is always with us. He holds us by the hand each minute. But spending time alone with him reminds us that in the dailiness and business of life, we can miss his hand.

"Father, prompt us to know that we cannot stand or walk on our own."

NOVEMBER
19

HYMN

Hold Thou my hand;   Without the sunlight

the way is dark before me   of Thy face divine;

SCRIPTURE

Even when I walk through the darkest valley, I will not be afraid, for you are close beside me. Your rod and your staff protect and comfort me (Psalm 23:4).

MEDITATION

In every cave tour I have been on, there is a time when the guide warns us and then turns out the lights. The darkness is overwhelming. You cannot see your hand in front of your face. The guide leaves the lights off for less than a minute, but it seems like forever.

There is much darkness in our world. Hunger, war, cruelty, and injustice. There is much darkness in our lives. Betrayal, disappointment, suffering, and doubt.

Our Shepherd leads us through the dark valley. He protects and comforts in the gloom. When we can see nothing else in the darkness, we see his face. He is the light of the world. He is the light of our life. He may not immediately take the dark away, but we feel his hand, especially in the dark.

"Loving Shepherd, may we know you are with us on our darkest days."

NOVEMBER
20

HYMN

But when by faith / I catch its radiant glory, / What heights of joy, / what rapturous songs are mine!

SCRIPTURE

So all of us who have had that veil removed can see and reflect the glory of the Lord. And the Lord—who is the Spirit—makes us more and more like him as we are changed into his glorious image (2 Corinthians 3:18).

MEDITATION

After many days of clouds and rain, we begin to wonder if we will ever see the sun. When the sun breaks through the clouds, we bask in its brightness and warmth. It's no wonder that ancient people worshipped the sun as the giver of life.

The true Giver of Life made the sun. His glory is brighter than the glory of the sun. And he shares that glory with us. When we experience the glow and warmth of his Presence, God changes us. We reflect his glory. We resemble our Father. We show his love, justice, and mercy to others. We break out in rapturous songs of praise to our God. And, by his grace, we become what we worship.

"Glorious God, may we shine forth with your light this day."

NOVEMBER
21

HYMN

Hold Thou my hand, / Of that lone river

that when I reach the margin / Thou didst cross for me,

SCRIPTURE

I want to know Christ and experience the mighty power that raised him from the dead. I want to suffer with him, sharing in his death, so that one way or another I will experience the resurrection from the dead! (Philippians 3:10-11).

MEDITATION

Death. Been there. Done that.

We have already died with Christ in baptism (Romans 6:1-11). So we should have no fear of death.

But we do. When we think of dying, our breathing becomes short, our hearts pound, and our bodies grow cold. We do not want to die!

Yes, we know we have already died with Christ. Yes, we believe that God raised him from the dead. Yes, we trust that God will also raise us up. Death is not the end. We die to be with the Lord. But still in the hour of our death, we need a hand to hold to.

"Lord, be with us as we cross the river of death."

NOVEMBER 22

HYMN

A heavenly light may flash along its waters,

And every wave like crystal bright shall be.

SCRIPTURE

Because God's children are human beings—made of flesh and blood—the Son also became flesh and blood. For only as a human being could he die, and only by dying could he break the power of the devil, who had the power of death. Only in this way could he set free all who have lived their lives as slaves to the fear of dying (Hebrews 2:14-15).

MEDITATION

We don't like to talk of death. We do not like to be around dead bodies. We have funeral homes to take care of them. We have rituals and euphemisms to keep us from speaking of death. People do not die, they "pass away," or "transition."

Jesus broke the power of death by his death and resurrection. The power of death is fear. When we cross the waters of death, the light of Jesus shines on the waters and lights our way. The end of life is not the darkness we fear but the Light Divine. So let us speak boldly of death, for Christ has set us free from its power. Death itself will die.

"Jesus, you faced the fear of death for us. Take our fear away."

NOVEMBER
23

HYMN

I thank Thee, Lord, that in Thy blood, My guilt is washed away;

SCRIPTURE

And since we have a great High Priest who rules over God's house, let us go right into the presence of God with sincere hearts fully trusting him. For our guilty consciences have been sprinkled with Christ's blood to make us clean, and our bodies have been washed with pure water (Hebrews 10:21-22).

MEDITATION

When we think of the blessings God has given us, so many things come to mind. But the greatest blessing of all is that God has restored our relationship to him. Nothing can separate us from his love.

But surely, we can separate ourselves from him. Although we are God's children, we continue to sin. Guilt and shame still stalk us.

They should not. We should trust the blood of Christ that he gave to cleanse our consciences once and for all. He took away our shame. Our guilt is washed away. All he asks of us is to accept his gift. He asks for a life of gratitude.

"Savior, we thank for our complete, once-for-all purification through your blood."

NOVEMBER
24

HYMN

I thank Thee that mine eyes behold   A bright and glorious day;

SCRIPTURE

The way of the righteous is like the first gleam of dawn, which shines ever brighter until the full light of day (Proverbs 4:18).

MEDITATION

Although blind, Fanny Crosby often writes of seeing in her hymns. Her physical eyes could not "behold a bright and glorious day," but she could still see it by faith.

Sight and faith are often contrasted in the Bible. "For we live by believing and not by seeing" (1 Corinthians 5:7). At other times, the Bible speaks of faith as a new way of seeing. "Faith shows the reality of what we hope for; it is the evidence of things we cannot see" (Hebrews 11:1).

By faith, Fanny Crosby could see what others could not see. So also with us. We can see the hand of a loving God when others can only see hardship and despair. We can see a hopeful future when others see only nightmarish prospects. We can see the bright and glorious day that God promises.

"God of light, open our eyes to the loveliness of this day."

NOVEMBER
25

HYMN

I thank Thee, Lord, for faith to see   A world of endless joy in Thee.

SCRIPTURE

But let all who take refuge in you rejoice; let them sing joyful praises forever. Spread your protection over them, that all who love your name may be filled with joy (Psalm 5:11).

MEDITATION

We long for happiness, but God promises more than that. He gives us joy.

Joy may seem briefer than happiness. We think of joy as a momentary experience. But the Bible uses joy to speak of that indescribable and lasting desire for God. We long for something that this life can never fully satisfy. Our thirst cannot be quenched. Our hunger cannot be filled. No matter how happy we are in this life, we know there is something more.

That "more" is God. There will come a time when we will see him face to face. A time when our desires will be fully satisfied. We often speak of that time beyond time as "heaven." That is when our joy will be complete.

But even now we catch glimpses of that day. By faith, we even see this life as a world of endless joy. For that, we give thanks.

"Lord God, may we desire you alone. Give us the joy of your Presence."

NOVEMBER
26

HYMN

I thank Thee for a throne of grace
Where Thou dost bend Thine ear,
And I may breathe my soul's request
When only Thou canst hear,

SCRIPTURE

But when you pray, go away by yourself, shut the door behind you, and pray to your Father in private. Then your Father, who sees everything, will reward you (Matthew 6:6).

MEDITATION

We are invited, even encouraged, to enter the Presence of the Almighty God.

When someone in the Bible encounters the Presence of God, they take off their shoes, fall on their faces, and fear for their lives. Who can enter the throne room of the Holy God? No one is worthy to be in His company.

But God calls us to be near him. He took on flesh to be near to us. Through the work of Jesus and the gift of the Spirit, we honestly pour out our hearts to the Holy God.

And he hears us! He understands us! He knows what it is like to be weak and helpless. We come to him boldly because we have heard his invitation to approach and receive a blessing.

"God who hears us, thank you for rewarding us with your nearness."

NOVEMBER
27

HYMN

I thank Thee for the hope of life   That looks beyond the tomb;

SCRIPTURE

This truth gives them confidence that they have eternal life, which God—who does not lie—promised them before the world began (Titus 1:2).

MEDITATION

Hope is not just for the future but for the present.

I have known Christians who thought so much about heaven that they were no earthly good. Placing all their attention on God's future made them complacent about the world they live in now.

On the other hand, some followers of Jesus act as if this world was the only one. They either live for the pleasure, power, and fame of our culture or they think improving society is completely up to them.

Biblical hope turns our eyes to a richer life beyond the tomb. It also opens our eyes to the work of God in the current world. God works through us to help the poor, heal the sick, and free the prisoners because that is the way it will be in the world to come.

"Jesus, you overcame death to give us life now and forever. Thank you for that gift."

NOVEMBER
28

HYMN

I thank Thee for the light that shines   To cheer me thro' its gloom;

SCRIPTURE

Jesus spoke to the people once more and said, "I am the light of the world. If you follow me, you won't have to walk in darkness, because you will have the light that leads to life" (John 8:12).

MEDITATION

When I get up at night, I don't want to turn on the light and disturb my wife, so I have to feel my way in the dark. I'm familiar enough with the room that I usually have no trouble. But I have the bumps and bruises to prove that I sometimes collide with walls and furniture.

Light is not an end in itself. We need light to see how to walk.

When Jesus says he is the light of the world, he implies that his light gives warmth and safety. But he says the purpose of his light is to show us where to walk. We have a calling, a responsibility, to follow the path that Jesus pioneered. That path leads to death, then life, through resurrection. We follow not only at the time of our deaths, but each moment of each day.

God has given us the ability to respond to the light of Jesus. Step by step he leads us. Let us not be distracted by the gloom around us but open our eyes to the light.

"Light of the World, shine on our path today."

NOVEMBER
29

HYMN

And Lord, for all Thy gifts to me, My loudest praise I give to Thee.

SCRIPTURE

Come, let us sing to the Lord! Let us shout joyfully to the Rock of our salvation. Let us come to him with thanksgiving. Let us sing psalms of praise to him (Psalm 95:1-2).

MEDITATION

"Let's go around the table and tell what we are thankful for." That's our tradition for Thanksgiving Day. Perhaps you have the same ritual.

It is a great practice for every day. Take a moment now to name five things for which you are thankful. When the day gets busy, reflect on those blessings. When the day gets hard, think on them again. When you feel sorry for yourself, repeat that list of blessings. Rehearse them when someone slights you.

This is not just an exercise in positive thinking. It is a reminder of the way things really are. We can easily let our busy moments, our profound disappointments, and our constant worries blind us to the reality of a God who pours blessings on us.

When we remember those blessings, we erupt with loud praise!

"We shout! We sing! We thank you, giving God, for all your blessings."

NOVEMBER
30

HYMN

O dawn of peace and gladness,
That breaks from sea to sea!
Behold it shine with joy divine
On ancient Galilee;

SCRIPTURE

"Because of God's tender mercy, the morning light from heaven is about to break upon us, to give light to those who sit in darkness and in the shadow of death, and to guide us to the path of peace" (Luke 1:78-79).

MEDITATION

After the angel Gabriel tells Mary she will have a child from the Holy Spirit, she breaks out in song. Called the "Magnificat" after the first line in the Latin Bible (*Magnificat anima mea Dominum* or "My Soul magnifies the Lord"), her song ties the news of her pregnancy to all the promises of God to his people.

Mary does not fully know what Jesus will accomplish, but she knows the Lord's mercy towards her will bring a revolution that humbles the proud and mighty and exalts the hungry and poor. She catches a glimpse of the dawn of that new age of light, peace, gladness, and joy. With Mary, let us magnify the name of the Lord!

"Father, you brought us light from a humble woman. Give us the light of Jesus today!"

DECEMBER 1

HYMN

For Judah's star is risen!   The Lord, the King Immanuel,

Her night is passed away!   Is born this holy day!

SCRIPTURE

The scepter will not depart from Judah, nor the ruler's staff from his descendants, until the coming of the one to whom it belongs, the one whom all nations will honor (Genesis 49:10).

MEDITATION

When David wanted to build a house, a temple, for God, the Lord instead says he will build a house, a dynasty, for David. God promises that dynasty of kings will last forever (see 2 Samuel 7:11-16). Yet David's dynasty did not last. Israel and Judah are conquered and taken into exile. Later they are under the rule of Greece and Rome, with no Davidic king to rule.

But even then, they trust God's promise of the restoration of Israel. A king from the line of David will rule again. The scepter will not depart from Judah, the tribe of David. God will send another anointed one ("Messiah") who will reign with power and justice. When those in the Gospels call Jesus, "Son of David," they are not simply commenting on his ancestry. They are claiming the promise to Judah and to David.

"Lord God, we rejoice in your promise-keeping to your people."

DECEMBER 2

HYMN

O dawn of peace and gladness,
That thrills the heart of earth!
When bells of joy their tones employ
To tell a Savior's birth,

SCRIPTURE

On that day even the harness bells of the horses will be inscribed with these words: Holy to the lord. And the cooking pots in the Temple of the Lord will be as sacred as the basins used beside the altar (Zechariah 14:20).

MEDITATION

We associate church bells with Christmas and the birth of the Messiah.

There are bells on the hem of the robe of Aaron (Exodus 28:33-35) and bells on the harnesses of horse in this verse from Zechariah. Those are the only bells in the Bible.

The Zechariah verse points to a time when God restores his people, and everything will be sacred. Horses will not be used for battle but for service to the Lord. Ordinary pots will be as holy as temple vessels.

It may be a stretch, but when the bells chime for the birth of Jesus, they mark a time when, through the work of Jesus, everything becomes Holy to the Lord.

"Lord make every part of our lives holy to you."

DECEMBER 3

HYMN

When hill and plain and valley
Repeat the angels' cry,
And sing in mighty chorus,
All praise to God most high!

SCRIPTURE

Suddenly, the angel was joined by a vast host of others—the armies of heaven—praising God and saying, "Glory to God in highest heaven, and peace on earth to those with whom God is pleased" (Luke 2:13-14).

MEDITATION

We have reflected before on the song of angels. These messengers praise God from eternity to eternity.

Yet this is a special angel song. It is a song of proclamation, "a Savior is born." We join this song by proclaiming the good news that God became flesh. Like the angels, we announce that news to rich and poor, lowly and great. We invite all we know to follow the example of the shepherds who first heard the angel song. Like them, everyone should go and see Jesus for themselves. Then they and the whole creation will share in declaring that news and singing that praise. Glory to God! Peace on earth!

"Father, we praise you for the gift of a Savior. May we know your pleasure."

DECEMBER 4

HYMN

O dawn of peace and gladness,
We read the holy sign;

The tidings sweet our tongues repeat
In songs of praise divine;

SCRIPTURE

The Lord himself will give you the sign. Look! The virgin will conceive a child! She will give birth to a son and will call him Immanuel (which means "God is with us") (Isaiah 7:14).

MEDITATION

In the Bible, signs are tricky things. Sometimes God tells his people to ask for signs. At other times, he condemns them for not trusting him unless they get a sign. What is a sign to one person means nothing to another. Signs must be interpreted. And one sign can have two meanings.

So it is with this sign. When given in the time of Isaiah, the sign is not of a virgin birth, but of a young woman who has a child named Immanuel. The sign is that before the child is old enough to know right from wrong, God will send destruction on King Ahaz and Israel. But the sign has a second, deeper meaning. A virgin will give birth to a child who is the ultimate Immanuel "God with us." That is the sign we must read.

"Lord God, open our eyes to the sign of your Presence with us."

DECEMBER
5

HYMN

For Judah's star is risen!
Let Zion's host proclaim;
All hail the Son of David,
O magnify His name!

SCRIPTURE

The crowd was amazed and asked, "Could it be that Jesus is the Son of David, the Messiah?" (Matthew 12:23).

MEDITATION

David, the great king. David, the "man after God's own heart" (1 Samuel 13:14). David, who covets, commits adultery, steals a man's wife, and murders him.

Is Jesus exactly like David? Yes and no. Like David, Jesus knows the power of temptation. However, he does not give in to the temptation. "He faced all of the same testings we do, yet he did not sin" (Hebrews 4:15).

In Matthew, the crowd thinks Jesus is the Son of David because he heals a man who cannot see nor speak. He has the power of God, as David did. He trusts in God, as David did. But even before he conquers temptation and does amazing miracles, when he is a helpless baby in a manger, we see the one who will be a greater King than David.

"Jesus, Son of David, we magnify your Name! Heal our weakness this day."

DECEMBER 6

HYMN

I know not the hour of his coming,

Nor how he will speak to my heart;

Or whether at morning or midday

My spirit to him will depart.

SCRIPTURE

"So you, too, must keep watch! For you do not know the day or hour of my return" (Matthew 25:13).

MEDITATION

In speaking of "not knowing the hour," Fanny J. Crosby refers to two events. One is the Second Coming of Jesus. At this time of the year, we focus primarily on the first coming of Jesus, his coming in the flesh of the baby born in Bethlehem. In that child, God with us, we see all the hopes of God's people begin to be fulfilled.

We also anticipate the second advent of Christ, when he will bring a new heaven and earth that completely fulfills our hope. How do we prepare ourselves for that Second Coming, since we do not know when it will be? Do we constantly repeat, "Today might be the day"? Today would be a good day for his return, but I'm not sure we can keep that in the forefront of our minds at all times. What we can do is live in a way that counts on his coming.

"Lord Jesus, come quickly and renew the world."

DECEMBER

7

HYMN

I know not the bliss that awaits me,
At rest with my Savior above;
I know not how soon I shall enter,
And bathe in the ocean of love.

SCRIPTURE

Yes, we are fully confident, and we would rather be away from these earthly bodies, for then we will be at home with the Lord (2 Corinthians 5:8).

MEDITATION

Along with the return of Jesus, the second event where we do not know the hour is the time of our death. That is the primary focus of this hymn. Jesus certainly may return in our lifetime, but it seems more likely that we will see Jesus after our deaths before we see him appear in glory.

We'd like to know more clearly what happens when we die. Until the resurrection we will be disembodied. What will that be like? We rest in death. The Bible often speaks of death as sleep. So will be conscious? Will we immediately be with those we love who have preceded us in death? Or will that happen only on resurrection day? I don't have answers to these questions. All we need to know is that when we die, we go to be with the Lord.

"Lord Jesus, may I trust that I will see your face after death."

DECEMBER 8

HYMN

Perhaps in the midst of my labor
A voice from my Lord I shall hear;

Perhaps in the slumber of midnight
Its message will fall on my ear.

SCRIPTURE

If we live, it's to honor the Lord. And if we die, it's to honor the Lord. So whether we live or die, we belong to the Lord (Romans 14:8).

MEDITATION

"In the midst of life we are in death."

That's a line from a Gregorian chant of the 14th Century. To our ears it sounds so medieval, so out of touch with the world we live in. It is morbid and depressing. We surely don't need that.

Yet it is true. We do not know the hour of our death, so the possibility of dying is always with us. We can ignore that fact. We can face it with cynicism as if nothing matters in light of death. We can let the fear of death drive us into depression or anger.

Jesus calls us to a healthier and more realistic response. Since we do not know the time of our death, we make every minute count for him. And we listen for his voice.

"Lord Jesus, may we make this day count, knowing it may be our last."

DECEMBER 9

HYMN

I know not, but oh, I am watching,
My lamp ever burning and bright,

I know not if Jesus will call me
At morning, at noon, or at night.

SCRIPTURE

"Arise, Jerusalem! Let your light shine for all to see. For the glory of the Lord rises to shine on you" (Isaiah 60:1).

MEDITATION

Jesus warns us to be ready for his coming because we do not know when it will be. This warning comes at the end of a story of ten bridesmaids waiting for the arrival of a bridegroom. A delay in his arrival until midnight means that five of them burn up all the oil in their lamps and cannot find him. Five others thought ahead, brought extra oil, and enjoy the wedding feast.

How do we stay ready for the coming of Jesus? We prepare. We think ahead. We try to anticipate every eventuality. This story is not about oil, but about the preparation of our hearts.

The lamps are important part of the story. Jesus tells us "In the same way, let your good deeds shine out for all to see, so that everyone will praise your heavenly Father" (Matthew 5:16). We wait on Jesus by pointing others to the Light of the world.

"Jesus, Light of the world, shine out from our hearts to those around us."

DECEMBER
10

HYMN

But I know I shall wake in the likeness

Of him I am longing to see;

I know that mine eyes shall behold him,

And that is enough for me.

SCRIPTURE

Dear friends, we are already God's children, but he has not yet shown us what we will be like when Christ appears. But we do know that we will be like him, for we will see him as he really is (1 John 3:2).

MEDITATION

We will be like Jesus. What does that mean?

This might be a hint of what our resurrection bodies will be like. After his resurrection, Jesus has a body that can be seen and touched. He continues to eat in his resurrected body. On the other hand, there are times when those who know him do not recognize him after the resurrection. He appears and disappears at will. So is his resurrection body like his body before death? Yes and no.

Will our bodies after the resurrection be like our current bodies? Yes and no. The good news is, like the body of Jesus, they will no longer grow old and die. We are raised immortal.

"Jesus, we want to see you. We want to be like you. Come quickly!"

DECEMBER
11

HYMN

Like the sound of many waters
Rolling on through ages long;
In a tide of rapture breaking—
Hark! the mighty choral song!

SCRIPTURE

Suddenly, the glory of the God of Israel appeared from the east. The sound of his coming was like the roar of rushing waters, and the whole landscape shone with his glory (Ezekiel 43:2).

MEDITATION

I love waterfalls. When you take a hike to a falls, you can hear the water long before you see it. When you arrive, the noise is deafening. The power of the water overwhelms.

So it is with the glory of God. Even when we seem far away from his Presence, we can hear him from a distance. When we grow closer, he drowns us in his glory.

Think of God and water in the Bible. God divides the water in creation. He judges and saves through water in the flood. He gives water to his people from a rock in the wilderness. When God becomes flesh, Jesus turns water into wine. He promises living water to a woman at a well. He tells us the Spirit will be in us like a fountain of water. He commands baptism in water in the name of Father, Son, and Spirit. The New Jerusalem comes with the river of life.

"Loving God, drown us in your glory and love this day."

DECEMBER
12

HYMN

Lo! the Morning Star appeareth,
O'er the world, His beams are cast;

He the Alpha and Omega,
He the Great, the First, the Last.

SCRIPTURE

Because of that experience, we have even greater confidence in the message proclaimed by the prophets. You must pay close attention to what they wrote, for their words are like a lamp shining in a dark place—until the Day dawns, and Christ the Morning Star shines in your hearts (2 Peter 1:19).

MEDITATION

The morning star is the last star we see before dawn comes. To call Jesus our Morning Star is to confess that the dawn of heaven is about to break.

The prophets spoke of the dawn of a new age. We should pay close attention to their words because they shine with the light of God. The Lord has not abandoned his people, even though they abandoned him. The prophets say he is sending a brighter light, as bright as the sun.

When Jesus is born, the Light of the World begins to shine. When he returns, in the new Jerusalem there will be no need of sun or moon, for the Glory of God and the Lamb gives light.

"Light of the World, shine on us now. May you light our eternity!"

DECEMBER 13

HYMN

Clap your hands with exultation!
Sing aloud, rejoice with mirth,

Peace her silver wing hath folded:
Lo! she comes to dwell on earth!

SCRIPTURE

Oh, that I had wings like a dove, then I would fly away and rest! I would fly far away to the quiet of the wilderness (Psalm 55:6-7).

MEDITATION

Doves are symbols of peace.

When Noah sends a dove from the ark after the flood, it returns with an olive branch in its mouth, a sign of new beginnings and new hope for humanity (Genesis 8:10-12).

When Jesus is baptized, the Holy Spirit descends on him in the form of a dove, a sign of the approval and power of God (Luke 3:21-22).

The Psalm above longs to escape to a place of rest and peace on the wings of a dove.

The hymn portrays the birth of Jesus as the coming of the Prince of Peace. He comes on the silver wings of a dove to bring peace to a divided world and to troubled hearts.

"Father, send your Dove of peace into our lives this day."

DECEMBER 14

HYMN

Savior, not with costly treasure
Do we gather at Thy throne,

All we have, our hearts we give Thee,
Consecrate them Thine alone.

SCRIPTURE

For it is by believing in your heart that you are made right with God, and it is by openly declaring your faith that you are saved (Romans 10:10).

MEDITATION

The wise men brought expensive gifts to Jesus as the newborn king of the Jews—gold, frankincense, and myrrh.

There is a story of a tribe who made their church contributions by goods instead of money. On Sunday, they would draw a large circle on the ground. They would then place their gifts to God—a chicken, crops, clothing or something else of value—in the circle. One Sunday a man walked into the circle and sat down. The tribe asked, "What are you doing?" The man answered, "I have nothing of value but myself. I give myself to God."

We bring King Jesus one gift—our whole life. That is the gift he desires more than any other.

"We give you all that we have, all that we are, King Jesus. Accept our sincere hearts."

DECEMBER 15

HYMN

Hallelujah! Hallelujah!
Let the heav'nly portals ring!
Christ is born, the Prince of glory!
Christ the Lord, our mighty King!

SCRIPTURE

Who is the King of glory? The Lord, strong and mighty; the Lord, invincible in battle (Psalm 24:8).

MEDITATION

I have worshipped with Christians in many countries. Often, I could not understand a word of their language. Except for one word.

"Hallelujah!" In every land they knew and used this Hebrew word. "Hallelu" meaning "let us praise." "Jah," the name of the Lord, Yahweh. Every minute somewhere around the world there are people saying "Hallelujah," praising the Lord, the King of glory. When we sing and shout "Hallelujah", we join with human voices but also with the voices of angels and all creation.

At the birth of Jesus, we join in the "Hallelujah!" When he comes triumphantly into Jerusalem, we add our voice to the adoring crowd. When he comes from the tomb we shout it. When he returns, we will sing praise to the Lamb for all eternity.

"Hallelujah! We give praise to the King of glory."

DECEMBER 16

HYMN

Hark! the mighty tones sublime,
Trumpet tongues of olden time—
Breathing on the silent air,
Shouting glory everywhere!

SCRIPTURE

The trumpeters and singers performed together in unison to praise and give thanks to the Lord. Accompanied by trumpets, cymbals, and other instruments, they raised their voices and praised the Lord with these words: "He is good! His faithful love endures forever!" At that moment a thick cloud filled the Temple of the Lord (2 Chronicles 5:13).

MEDITATION

Trumpets announce and celebrate the dedication of the temple by Solomon and God's people. The climax of that day was the thick cloud symbolizing the glory of the Lord that filled the temple. God's presence would be with his people.

The hymn pictures the angels who announced the coming of Jesus to the shepherds as singing with trumpet tones from older times. Once God's presence filled the temple. Now it completely fills the baby in the manger in Bethlehem. God has created a new and ultimate temple, the body of the Word made flesh. Later Jesus will call his body a temple (John 2:19-22).

"Jesus, temple of the living God, may we trumpet the news of your birth!"

DECEMBER
17

HYMN

Hark! again their joyful sound
Rings afar, the earth around;
While a vast, adoring throng,
Catch the strain and join the song.

SCRIPTURE

And they were singing the song of Moses, the servant of God, and the song of the Lamb: "Great and marvelous are your works, O Lord God, the Almighty. Just and true are your ways, O King of the nations" (Revelation 15:3).

MEDITATION

Angels sing at the birth of Jesus.

That song continues. Throughout the ages and today, countless followers of Jesus have lifted their voices to proclaim glory to God and peace on earth.

The song goes back to Moses who sang of God's deliverance of his people from slavery in Egypt (Exodus 15). Near the end of his life, Moses sings another song praising the faithfulness of God (Deuteronomy 32).

The song will continue for eternity. The verse from Revelation tells of those who triumphed over evil singing the song of Moses and the song of the Lamb.

"Faithful God, we add our voices of praise to you for your gift of a Son."

DECEMBER 18

HYMN

Mourning captive, cease thy tears;
Lo! the promised day appears,
Through the misty vail of night,
Bursting in a flood of light;

SCRIPTURE

To all who mourn in Israel, he will give a crown of beauty for ashes, a joyous blessing instead of mourning, festive praise instead of despair. In their righteousness, they will be like great oaks that the Lord has planted for his own glory (Isaiah 61:3).

MEDITATION

When we look at the state of the world, we cannot help but mourn. Corruption, poverty, and violence confront us on every side. We mourn our own captivity to a fallen culture.

We do not ignore the state of the world, but we also see a deeper reality. We believe that two thousand years ago a child was born who ended corruption, made the poor rich, and brought peace to a war-torn world. He freed us all from captivity.

It does not look like that yet. But we trust the promises of God—beauty instead of ashes, joy instead of mourning, and praise instead of despair. This is not wishful thinking but a firm conviction that the promised day has come and will come.

"Father, flood us with the light of Jesus in the midst of the darkness around us."

DECEMBER
19

HYMN

Oh, what wondrous things are done
By the Father, through the Son!

Oh, the smile of pard'ning grace,
Beaming in the Saviour's face!

SCRIPTURE

So Jesus explained, "I tell you the truth, the Son can do nothing by himself. He does only what he sees the Father doing. Whatever the Father does, the Son also does" (John 5:19).

MEDITATION

The Trinity is a mystery. We cannot comprehend the relationship among Father, Son, and Spirit who are one God.

Jesus says he does only what the Father does. Jesus does not claim power for himself but always speaks of the Father working through him. God gave his Spirit to Jesus at baptism to empower him.

Jesus also says he will work in his followers through the Spirit (John 16:5-15). Like Jesus, we receive the empowering Spirit at baptism (Acts 2:38).

So who works in us? The Spirit? Jesus? The Father? Yes! Yes to all! And so we praise the Father for the wonderous things he does through the Son and Spirit. To God alone be the glory!

"Savior, may we see the face of God in all we do this day."

DECEMBER
20

HYMN

Now with healing in her wings,
Hark! a white robed angel sings:—

"Mortals from the realms above,
I have borne my harp of love;"

SCRIPTURE

"But for you who fear my name, the Sun of Righteousness will rise with healing in his wings. And you will go free, leaping with joy like calves let out to pasture" (Malachi 4:2).

MEDITATION

"Healing in his wings." What does that mean? Some say it refers to the wings or rays of the sun with its healing power. In the hymn, Fanny Crosby associates the healing with the wings of the angel who announces the birth of Jesus.

Some associate the phrase with the story of Jesus healing the woman with the hemorrhage (Matthew 9:20–22, Mark 5:25–34, and Luke 8:43–48). She thought, "If only I can touch the fringe of his robe, I can be healed." So she touches and immediately her bleeding stops. What made her think of the fringe of his robe? Perhaps she was thinking of the verse from Malachi. "Wings" can also mean "edge of a garment" in Hebrew. Perhaps it is a stretch, but I like to think of the Sun of Righteousness being the Son who heals the world.

"Lord, give us the trust of this woman, trust in your healing power."

DECEMBER 21

HYMN

"Hallelujah! sing with me; Sing, in purest, sweetest lays,
Hail our greatest jubilee! On this holy day of days."

SCRIPTURE

But the angel reassured them. "Don't be afraid!" he said. "I bring you good news that will bring great joy to all people. The Savior—yes, the Messiah, the Lord—has been born today in Bethlehem, the city of David!" (Luke 2:10-11).

MEDITATION

We love holidays. Holiday means time off from work or school. Holiday means vacation and trips with the family. That's why we celebrate holidays.

But originally holiday meant "holy day." It was not simply a day off, but an observance of an event with holy significance. The birth of Jesus is certainly such a day, the day when the Holy One became one of us.

So even though we do not know the date of his birth, it is proper to designate a season and a day for a festival, not just of family and fun, but to praise God for the greatest gift of all. To us a Savior is born.

"Lord, bless our joyful merrymaking at the birth of your Son."

DECEMBER 22

HYMN

Unto us a child is given;

Open now the gates of heaven;

Eden lost, to man restored,

Through the birth of Christ the Lord.

SCRIPTURE

For the sin of this one man, Adam, caused death to rule over many. But even greater is God's wonderful grace and his gift of righteousness, for all who receive it will live in triumph over sin and death through this one man, Jesus Christ (Romans 5:17).

MEDITATION

Think of what we lost. God made humans to have fellowship with him. He placed us in a paradise. He provided everything we needed for life.

Then we blew it. We turned our backs on God and he turned us out of the Garden of Eden. But the Lord did not abandon us. He called Abraham. He created a people to serve him. Even when they rebelled against him, he made an even greater promise of reclamation for humanity. In Jesus, he took on flesh, became part of us, and bought us with his blood. He has more in store for us than what we lost. Through Jesus we will have Eden restored, a new Jerusalem with the river of life flowing through it. A city where the living God will walk with us.

"God of love, you made us for yourself, may we walk this day with you."

DECEMBER 23

HYMN

In a lowly manger sleeping,
Calm and still a Babe we see,
'Tis the Holy Child of promise,
Light of all the world is He.

SCRIPTURE

She gave birth to her firstborn son. She wrapped him snugly in strips of cloth and laid him in a manger, because there was no lodging available for them (Luke 2:7).

MEDITATION

Several years ago, in another country, a woman invited me and others to visit her home after church. She was quite proud of the improvements she had made to her house. It was one of the poorest homes I had ever been to, with a bare concrete floor and thin walls for protection from the weather. I felt that way because of my middle-class upbringing in the United States.

I wonder if the shepherds who first saw Jesus had a similar reaction. Sure, shepherds were not wealthy, but they probably had a better cradle for their newborn babies than a feeding trough. Yet in that manger was the treasure of the world.

I sincerely thanked the woman for her hospitality and shared her joy in the upgrade to her house. Jesus still lives in humble abodes.

"Jesus, thank you for living in humble places and humble hearts."

DECEMBER
24

HYMN

Holy angels sing His welcome In the realms of glory bright, While the morning stars around Him Fall in soft and tender light.

SCRIPTURE

Then Jesus called for the children and said to the disciples, "Let the children come to me. Don't stop them! For the Kingdom of God belongs to those who are like these children" (Luke 18:16).

MEDITATION

Fanny Crosby wrote this hymn for children. That's why the words are so simple.

We associate Christmas with children. Many churches still have a Christmas pageant where children act out the story of the birth of Jesus. Combining the stories from Matthew and Luke, there are roles for Mary and Joseph, shepherds, angels, and wise men. I once heard the story of a little boy who was trying out for a role in the Christmas pageant. His mother was nervous because he did not have much acting talent. But he came home excited from Sunday School, saying "I got a part in the pageant!" His mother asked, "What part?" "I've been chosen to clap and cheer," he replied with a beaming smile.

Angels and stars sing at his birth. We get to clap and cheer.

"Generous Father, may we receive your gift of Jesus with joy like children do."

DECEMBER 25

HYMN

Blessèd Savior, dear Redeemer,
King of Judah, Prince of Peace,
Rock of Ages, Star of nations,
Thy dominion ne'er shall cease.

SCRIPTURE

"He will be very great and will be called the Son of the Most High. The Lord God will give him the throne of his ancestor David. And he will reign over Israel forever; his Kingdom will never end!" (Luke 1:31-32).

MEDITATION

Among the thousands of her hymns, Fanny Crosby never wrote a famous Christmas carol, the ones we sing every year. But in this one stanza, she encapsulates most of the themes of advent.

Jesus is the blessed Savior. When we were in danger, he saved our lives. Jesus is the dear Redeemer. He paid the price to free us from slavery to sin. Jesus is the King of Judah, the promised one who rules with mercy and justice. Jesus is the Prince of Peace to a violent, war-torn world. Jesus is the Rock of Ages, the one on whom we can depend. Jesus is the star that gives light to every nation. Jesus rules forever!

"Jesus, you are all this and more to us. We celebrate your birth!"

DECEMBER
26

HYMN

'Tis the blessed hour of prayer, when our hearts lowly bend,

And we gather to Jesus, our Savior and Friend;

If we come to Him in faith, His protection to share,

What a balm for the weary! O how sweet to be there!

SCRIPTURE

I hurt with the hurt of my people. I mourn and am overcome with grief. Is there no medicine in Gilead? Is there no physician there? Why is there no healing for the wounds of my people? (Jeremiah 8:21-22).

MEDITATION

Balm is medicine. When we hurt deeply for friends that are wounded, we cry out, "Can't anyone help them? Is there no cure or even relief for this pain?" That's the wound Jeremiah suffers for his people who have rejected God and experienced his punishment.

There is a remedy for the agony we face. In our desperation, we cry out to the Lord.

And he hears! In the blessed hour of prayer, we meet the Great Physician. He gave himself as the antidote for pain, suffering, and sin. When we make the time to be with him in prayer each day, it is a balm, a healing, a blessed hour with our Friend.

"Jesus, heal us. Share our pain. Take away our guilt and shame. Bless us!"

DECEMBER 27

HYMN

'Tis the blessed hour of prayer, when the Savior draws near,

With a tender compassion His children to hear;

When He tells us we may cast at His feet every care,

What a balm for the weary! O how sweet to be there!

SCRIPTURE

Give all your worries and cares to God, for he cares about you (1 Peter 5:7).

MEDITATION

I sometimes don't want to bother Jesus with my little problems. God has the whole world to take care of.

Then I realize that my little problems are not little to me. My mom has a cold. At her age, that could be serious. My bank has messed up my checking account. The hot water heater went out. I have a strange pain in my side. All little problems but they happen all at once.

Nothing is too big to take to Jesus. Nothing is too small. He lived on this earth with the daily cares we all face. He understands how we can obsess over tiny things. Every care, every nagging worry, we can take to him. We leave those anxieties at his feet. He is big enough to handle them all.

"Jesus, be with us in all things this day, great or small."

DECEMBER
28

HYMN

'Tis the blessed hour of prayer, when the tempted and tried

To the Savior who loves them their sorrows confide;

SCRIPTURE

The temptations in your life are no different from what others experience. And God is faithful. He will not allow the temptation to be more than you can stand. When you are tempted, he will show you a way out so that you can endure (1 Corinthians 10:13).

MEDITATION

Jesus taught us to pray, "And do not lead us to temptation but deliver us from evil."

Yet we find ourselves often in the time of trial and temptation. Sometimes the temptation is so subtle we give in before we know it. At other times we fight our urges hard but lose the battle. God promises to show us a way out of temptation, but often I cannot see the way.

Prayer is one sure help in temptation. We often have a painful struggle to overcome the sins that beset us. Jesus knows that struggle. We can confide our deepest and darkest secrets to him, knowing that he fights with us. His Spirit groans with us. His blood covers all our sin.

Even when prayer is painfully honest, it is a blessed hour with Jesus.

"Father, keep us from the time of trial. Jesus, be with us in our brawl with temptation."

DECEMBER 29

HYMN

With a sympathizing heart   What a balm for the weary!

He removes every care;   O how sweet to be there!

SCRIPTURE

Since he himself has gone through suffering and testing, he is able to help us when we are being tested (Hebrews 2:18).

MEDITATION

God cares for us—Father, Son, and Spirit.

It does not always feel that way. Even Jesus felt that way. "My God, my God, why have you forsaken me?"

When we feel that God has abandoned us, that he is not listening, and that our prayers go no higher than the ceiling, we take comfort in the truth that Jesus felt that way too. He can sympathize. He understands. But even when he felt that way, he still kept his trust in God. "Not my will, but yours be done."

And God did not abandon Jesus. He raised him from the dead. He will never leave us.

"Jesus, draw near to us. May we know you care for us, even when we do not feel it."

DECEMBER 30

HYMN

'Tis the blessed hour of prayer, That the blessings we're needing
trusting Him we believe, we'll surely receive;

SCRIPTURE

"You can pray for anything, and if you have faith, you will receive it" (Matthew 21:22).

MEDITATION

"I've stopped praying."

The words surprised me. They came from a deeply committed Christian woman. She went on to tell me that she had prayed for months that her young granddaughter would be healed. The granddaughter died. So what's the use of praying?

It takes great faith to continue to pray when we pray for what we want most and do not receive it. It is hard to trust a God who does not answer. There are times when prayer is not a blessed hour, but an hour to pour out our anger and disappointment toward God.

This woman did not give up on God forever. She later returned to prayer. She came to see that God through Christ is always listening. She recovered her trust. May we also.

"Jesus, increase our trust when faith is weak. May we never give up on your blessings."

DECEMBER 31

HYMN

In the fullness of this trust

we shall lose every care;

What a balm for the weary!

O how sweet to be there!

SCRIPTURE

Don't worry about anything; instead, pray about everything. Tell God what you need and thank him for all he has done. Then you will experience God's peace, which exceeds anything we can understand. His peace will guard your hearts and minds as you live in Christ Jesus (Philippians 4:6-7).

MEDITATION

Lately, I've begun to walk for my health. The first mile or so is still painful. But (and I never thought I'd say this) after a while walking makes me feel good.

So also with a daily quiet time with God.

I end this book with this hymn from Fanny Crosby, because it affirms the benefits of spending time alone with God each day. My prayer is that singing a hymn, meditating on the Bible, and spending time in prayer has been a blessing to you.

If so then let us continue in the new year to receive that blessing.

"God of love, draw us nearer to you each day."

INDEX OF HYMNS

A Little Talk with Jesus. January 1

A Wonderful Savior. August 13-17

All the Way My Savior Leads Me. March 12-17

As the Bird Flies Home. July 6-10

Awake! for the Trumpet Is Sounding! February 2-5.

Blessed Assurance. January 2-5

Blessed Redeemer. February 6-9

By Grace are Ye Saved. June 3-7

Christ Is Risen! March 27-30

Christ, the Lord, Is Risen Today! March 31-April 3

Come Boldly to the Throne of Grace. September 17-23

Come, Lord, and Let Thy Power. March 6-11

Conquering Now and Still to Conquer. May 20-23

Dwell in Me, O Blessed Spirit. September 8-12

Eye Hath Not Seen. July 31-August 4

From the Cross to the Crown. February 19-23.

God of Our Strength. July 22-25

Have Compassion, Lord, on Me! October 18-22

Have You Sought? June 17-24

He is Coming. December 6-10

He Is Coming. May 2-6

Heavenly Father, We Beseech Thee. January 29-February 1

Hold Thou My Hand. November 15-22

Holy Sabbath. May 16-19

Holy, Holy, Holy Is the Lord. January 15-17

I Am Thine, O Lord. June 8-12

I Know Not The Hour. December 6-10

I Thank Thee, Lord. November 23-29

In a Lowly Manger. December 23-25.

Jesus Is Tenderly Calling You Home. August 5-8

Jesus Keep Me Near the Cross. March 23-26

Judah's Star is Risen. November 30-December 5

Keep Me Ever Close to Thee. April 19-22

Let Your Light Shine Out. January 6-9

Like a Wayward Child. August 9-12

Like the Sound. December 11-15

More Like Jesus Would I Be. January 18-23

My Savior Knows. September 13-16

Never Be Afraid. May 7-11

No Book Is Like the Bible. June 25-July 1

No Voice but Thine. October 7-11

O Serve the Lord. July 11-17

One Blessed Hour with Jesus. August 27-31

Pass Me Not, O Gentle Savior. January 10-14

Praise Him, Praise Him. April 8-18

Praise Our Creator. September 30-October 3

Praise the Giver of All. June 13-16

Praise Ye the Lord. November 8-14

Redeemed, How I Love to Proclaim It. May 12-15

Rescue the Perishing. July 18-21

Sacred Fountain. May 24-28

Safe in the Arms of Jesus. September 24-29

Savior, More Than Life. April 23-26

Sing On. September 1-7.

Speak Not Harshly. October 12-17

Take the World, but Give Me Jesus. July 26-30

Tell Me the Story of Jesus. February 13-18

The Angel's Proclamation. December 16-22

The Lord in Zion Reigneth. February 10-12

The Pilgrim's Journey Words. January 24-28

There's a Friend That Abides. February 24-29

This Life is a Garden. October 23-27

Thou My Everlasting Portion. November 3-7

Thou Only Art Holy. October 28-November 2

Though Your Sins Be as Scarlet. October 4-6

Thy Holy Spirit, Lord, Alone. July 2-5

Tis the Blessed Hour of Prayer. December 26-31

To God Be the Glory. August 23-26

To the Work. May 29-June 2.

Tread Softly. August 18-22.

Trusting Jesus. April 4-7

We Cannot Fold Our Hands at Ease. March 18-22

When Jesus Comes to Reward His Servants. March 1-5

Will You Come? April 27-May 1

About Kharis Publishing:

Kharis Publishing, an imprint of Kharis Media LLC, is a leading Christian and inspirational book publisher based in Aurora, Chicago metropolitan area, Illinois. Kharis' dual mission is to give voice to under-represented writers (including women and first-time authors) and equip orphans in developing countries with literacy tools. That is why, for each book sold, the publisher channels some of the proceeds into providing books and computers for orphanages in developing countries so that these kids may learn to read, dream, and grow. For a limited time, Kharis Publishing is accepting unsolicited queries for nonfiction (Christian, self-help, memoirs, business, health and wellness) from qualified leaders, professionals, pastors, and ministers. Learn more at: https://kharispublishing.com/

www.ingramcontent.com/pod-product-compliance
Lightning Source LLC
Chambersburg PA
CBHW071225170426
43191CB00033B/1562